Professional React Native

Expert techniques and solutions for building high-quality, cross-platform, production-ready apps

Alexander Benedikt Kuttig

D1606906

BIRMINGHAM—MUMBAI

Professional React Native

Group Product Manager: Rohit Rajkumar

Publishing Product Manager: Nitin Nainani

Senior Editor: Hayden Edwards

Content Development Editor: Abhishek Jadhav

Technical Editor: Simran Ali

Copy Editor: Safis Editing

Project Coordinator: Sonam Pandey

Proofreader: Safis Editing

Indexer: Rekha Nair

Production Designer: Nilesh Mohite

Marketing Coordinator: Teny Thomas

First published: October 2022

Production reference: 1061022

Published by Packt Publishing Ltd.

Livery Place

35 Livery Street

Birmingham

B3 2PB, UK.

ISBN 978-1-80056-368-1

www.packt.com

To my wife, Karin, for her love, support, and inspiration. To my daughter, Leonie, for showing me how talent and creativity evolve every day. To my parents, Roswitha and Burkhard, and my brother, Dominik, for always being there for me. To my business partners, Werner and Philipp, for always having my back. And to all my colleagues for making my job absolutely awesome.

– Alexander Benedikt Kuttig

Contributors

About the author

Alexander Benedikt Kuttig has a master's degree in computer science and currently works as a software and app architect. With plenty of industry experience, he has created app architecture for different industries, such as education, sports and fitness, manufacturing, printing, and banking, which have been used by millions of users across the globe.

He runs multiple businesses, such as Horizon Alpha, an app development agency, and Teamfit, a digital corporate health platform. He also speaks about his work at different conferences, such as RNEU and the Geekle Cross-Platform Summit, and has a blog on Medium, which he uses to write about the challenges he faces. Alexander is highly experienced as a React Native developer, speaker, and contributor.

About the reviewer

Charles Mangwa is a weathered React Native expert who has been working with the framework for the past 7 years. His knowledge spans over, IoT focused projects, mobile DevOps and he also has published several open source libraries. While the whole React Native ecosystem is his tool of choice, whenever the JavaScript fatigue hits, he can be found working with Dart, building apps in Flutter.

Table of Contents

6

Working with Animations   109

7

Handling Gestures in React Native   133

8

JavaScript Engines and Hermes   149

9

Essential Tools for Improving React Native Development   157

Part 3: React Native in Large-Scale Projects and Organizations

10

Structuring Large-Scale, Multi-Platform Projects   173

11

Creating and Automating Workflows   193

12

Automated Testing for React Native Apps   209

13

Tips and Outlook   225

Preface

The React Native framework offers a range of powerful features that makes it possible to efficiently build high-quality, easy-to-maintain frontend applications across multiple platforms, such as iOS, Android, Linux, macOS X, Windows, and the web, helping you save both time and money.

In *Professional React Native*, you'll find the ultimate coverage of essential concepts, best practices, advanced processes, and easy-to-use tips for everyday developer problems. With step-by-step explanations, practical examples, and expert guidance, you'll understand how React Native works under the hood and then use this knowledge to develop highly performant apps. As you follow along, you'll learn the difference between React and React Native, navigate the React Native ecosystem, and revisit the basics of JavaScript and TypeScript that are needed to create a React Native application. You'll also work with animations and control your app with gestures. Finally, you'll be able to structure larger apps and improve developer efficiency through automated processes, testing, and continuous integration.

By the end of this React native app development book, you'll have gained the confidence to build high-performance apps for multiple platforms, even on a bigger scale.

Who this book is for

This book is for developers working with React Native interested in building professional cross-platform applications. Familiarity with the basics of JavaScript (including its syntax) and general software engineering concepts, including data types, control flows, and server/client structures, is required.

What this book covers

Chapter 1, *What Is React Native?*, will include a short introduction to React Native, how it is related to React and Expo, and how it is driven by the community.

Chapter 2, *Understanding the Essentials of JavaScript and TypeScript*, shows important underlying concepts to avoid the most common mistakes and bad patterns. You will get useful tips, learn best practices, and repeat the most important basics to use JavaScript in your apps.

Chapter 3, *Hello React Native*, will give you a deeper understanding of React Native. It contains core concepts, explained on an example app, as well as theoretical information about the architecture of React Native and how to connect different platforms to the React Native JavaScript bundle.

Chapter 4, Styling, Storage, and Navigation in React Native, covers different areas, which are all important to create a high-quality product with React Native. You have to focus on good user experience, which includes a good design and clear navigation. Also, your users should be able to use as much of your app as possible without a network connection, which means working with locally stored data.

Chapter 5, Managing States and Connecting Backends, focuses a lot on data. First, you will learn how to handle more complex data in your app. Then, we'll look at different options on how to make your app communicate with the rest of the world by connecting it to remote backends.

Chapter 6, Working with Animations, focuses on onscreen animations. There are multiple ways to achieve smooth animations in React Native. Depending on the type of project and animation you want to build, you can choose from a wide range of solutions, each with its own advantages and disadvantages. We will discuss the best and most widely used solutions in this chapter.

Chapter 7, Handling Gestures in React Native, teaches you how to work with gestures, how to combine gestures and animations, and what the best practices are to give user feedback.

Chapter 8, JavaScript Engines and Hermes, is mainly a theoretical chapter, where you will learn how different JavaScript Engines in React Native work and why Hermes is the preferred solution in production apps (when it is possible to use it). It includes some theoretical background as well as tests of key metrics in different environments.

Chapter 9, Essential Tools for Improving React Native Development, teaches you about useful tools that make development easier, especially when working on bigger projects. You will understand how Storybook works and why this is a great tool for React Native development. You will also learn about styled components for React Native, recommendations for different UI libraries, ESLint/TSLint, and boilerplate CLIs such as Ignite.

Chapter 10, Structuring Large-Scale, Multi-Platform Projects, teaches you how to structure a large-scale project. This includes the app architecture, processes for the successful collaboration of multiple developers, and processes to ensure good code quality.

Chapter 11, Creating and Automating Workflows, focuses exclusively on workflow automation. You will learn how to set up multiple CI pipelines for code quality checks, automated PR checks, automated communication via mail, Slack, or board issues, as well as automated deployment to the app stores. We will have a look at GitHub Actions, fastlane, Bitrise, and other CI/CD solutions.

Chapter 12, Automated Testing of React Native Apps, teaches you how to use Jest and the react-native-testing-library for unit and snapshot tests, how to ensure a certain test coverage, how to do E2E testing with Detox, and even how to test on real devices using AWS Device Farm and Appium.

Chapter 13, Tips and Outlook, is divided into two parts. In the first part, you can read my most useful tips on how to make your React Native project a success. The second part focuses on the outlook of the framework and how I think React Native, its community, and its ecosystem will develop in the future. This is based on technical development as well as commitment from different big players in the community.

To get the most out of this book

You should have a working React Native environment to be able to run the examples in this book. All examples are tested with React Native 0.68, but they should also work with future versions.

Software covered in the book	Operating system requirements
React Native 0.68	Windows, macOS, or Linux, preferably macOS
TypeScript 4.4	
ECMAScript 12	

If you are using the digital version of this book, we advise you to type the code yourself or access the code from the book's GitHub repository (a link is available in the next section). Doing so will help you avoid any potential errors related to the copying and pasting of code.

Download the example code files

You can download the example code files for this book from GitHub at `https://github.com/alexkuttig/prn-videoexample`. If there's an update to the code, it will be updated in the GitHub repository.

We also have other code bundles from our rich catalog of books and videos available at `https://github.com/PacktPublishing/`. Check them out!

Download the color images

We also provide a PDF file that has color images of the screenshots and diagrams used in this book. You can download it here: `https://packt.link/xPgoW`.

Conventions used

There are a number of text conventions used throughout this book.

`Code in text`: Indicates code words in text, database table names, folder names, filenames, file extensions, pathnames, dummy URLs, user input, and Twitter handles. Here is an example: "This is the `<Header />` component from our example project of the previous chapter but using inline styles to style the `Text` component."

A block of code is set as follows:

```
import React from 'react';
import {ScrollView, Text, View} from 'react-native';
const App = () => {
  return (
    <ScrollView contentInsetAdjustmentBehavior="automatic">
      <View>
        <Text>Hello World!</Text>
      </View>
    </ScrollView>
  );
};
```

When we wish to draw your attention to a particular part of a code block, the relevant lines or items are set in bold:

```
<Pressable
  key={genre.name}
  onPress={() => props.onGenrePress(genre)}
  testID={'test' + genre.name}>
  <Text style={styles.genreTitle}>{genre.name}</Text>
</Pressable>
```

Any command-line input or output is written as follows:

```
npx react-native init videoexample
    --template react-native-template-typescript
```

Bold: Indicates a new term, an important word, or words that you see onscreen. For instance, words in menus or dialog boxes appear in **bold**. Here is an example: "Go to **Settings**, scroll to the bottom, and choose **Developer**."

Tips or Important Notes
Appear like this.

Get in touch

Feedback from our readers is always welcome.

General feedback: If you have questions about any aspect of this book, email us at customercare@ packtpub.com and mention the book title in the subject of your message.

Errata: Although we have taken every care to ensure the accuracy of our content, mistakes do happen. If you have found a mistake in this book, we would be grateful if you would report this to us. Please visit www.packtpub.com/support/errata and fill in the form.

Piracy: If you come across any illegal copies of our works in any form on the internet, we would be grateful if you would provide us with the location address or website name. Please contact us at copyright@packt.com with a link to the material.

If you are interested in becoming an author: If there is a topic that you have expertise in and you are interested in either writing or contributing to a book, please visit authors.packtpub.com.

Share Your Thoughts

Once you've read *Professional React Native*, we'd love to hear your thoughts! Scan the QR code below to go straight to the Amazon review page for this book and share your feedback.

https://www.amazon.in/review/create-review/error?asin=180056368X

Your review is important to us and the tech community and will help us make sure we're delivering excellent quality content.

Part 1: Getting Started with React Native

This module is mainly for getting you to the needed level of basic knowledge of React and React Native to understand the more advanced modules, 2 and 3. After reading, you will understand how modern client development based on React works as well as the differences between React, React Native, and Expo.

The following chapters are in this section:

- *Chapter 1, What Is React Native?*
- *Chapter 2, Understanding the Essentials of JavaScript and TypeScript*
- *Chapter 3, Hello React Native*

1

What Is React Native?

Building high-quality apps for multiple platforms is the holy grail of app development. Since React Native was published, it has been challenged in very competitive environments because it seemed to be this holy grail for a long time. Its performance was much better than the performance of any of the competitors (Ionic, Cordova) back when it was released by Facebook in 2015 and its development speed is much faster than creating separate Android and iOS apps.

Since 2015, a lot has happened regarding React Native. Facebook open sourced the framework, a lot of contributors and even big companies such as Microsoft, Discord, and Shopify invested heavily in React Native, and new competitors such as Flutter of Kotlin Multiplatform Mobile evolved.

In 7 years, a lot of companies migrated their apps to React Native successfully, while others failed in doing so, migrated back to native development, or finally chose other multiplatform technologies.

In 2022, React Native is used in more products than ever and it has become a lot more developer friendly than in the early days. It is not only available for iOS and Android but also for macOS, Windows, web, VR, and other platforms. Most importantly, and despite many rumours claiming otherwise, Facebook is still betting heavily on React Native.

The React Native core team at Facebook just completed a rewrite of more than 1,000 React Native screens in its main application, including Dating, Jobs, and Marketplace, which is visited by more than 1 billion users each month. This means React Native powers important and business-critical parts of the biggest and most used app in the world, which is the ultimate proof of it being a stable and supported framework.

As you can see, React Native has become very powerful and is widely used. But you have to know how to leverage its strengths and how to deal with its weaknesses to create a high-quality app and a well-run software product. This book contains learnings, best practices, and basic architectural and processual concepts you need to know about to be able to decide on the following things:

- When to use React Native for your project
- How to set up your React Native project to work on a bigger scale

- How to use React Native to create a world-class product

- How to organize your team in a software project with React Native

- How to support your development team with useful tools and processes

This chapter contains a very brief introduction to the main concepts of React as the foundation on which React Native was built, of React Native itself, and of the Expo framework, which is a set of tools and libraries built on top of React Native. We will focus on the key concepts that are relevant for understanding the content that will be covered later in this book.

If you already have a very good understanding of how React, React Native, and Expo work, feel free to skip this chapter.

In this chapter, we will cover the following topics:

- Exploring React

- Understanding React basics

- Introducing React Native

- Introducing Expo

Technical requirements

To try out the code examples in this chapter, you need to set up a small React app for the *Exploring React* and *Understanding React basics* sections, and a React Native app for the *Introducing React Native* section. This requires you to install various libraries, depending on what OS you are working with. Both `https://reactjs.org/` and `https://reactnative.dev/` provide step-by-step guides for setting up the development environment correctly.

You can find the code in the book's GitHub repository:

Exploring React

On `https://reactjs.org/`, React is defined as a *JavaScript library for building user interfaces*. The main catchphrases used on the home page are declarative, component-based, and learn once, write anywhere.

When React was first introduced at the JSConf US conference in May 2013 by Jordan Walke of Facebook, the audience was so skeptical that Facebook decided to start a *React tour* to convince people of the benefits of this new library. Today, React is one of the most popular frameworks for creating web applications, and it's used not only by Facebook itself, but also by many other big players such as Instagram, Netflix, Microsoft, and Dropbox.

In the next section, I will show you how React works, what makes it so special compared to other similar frameworks and approaches, and how it is related to React Native.

> **Tip**
>
> If you already have Node and Node Package Manager installed, you can set up a new app by using the following command in the terminal:
>
> ```
> npx create-react-app name-of-your-app
> ```

Understanding React basics

To get started, open a project in your IDE so that we can explore a simple example. This is what a React app returning a simple `Hello World` message looks like:

```
function App() {
  return (
    <div>
      <p>Hello World!</p>
    </div>
  )
}
```

The first thing that comes to mind when seeing these code lines is probably that this looks just like XML/HTML! Indeed, it does, but these tags get converted into JavaScript by a preprocessor, so it's JavaScript code that looks like XML/HTML tags. Hence the name **JSX**, which is short for **JavaScript XML**.

The JSX tags can be used much like XML/HTML tags; you can structure your code using the different types of tags, and you can style them using CSS files and the `className` attribute, which is the React equivalent of HTML's `class` attribute.

On the other hand, you can insert JavaScript code anywhere in the JSX, either as a value for an attribute or inside a tag. You just have to put curly brackets around it. Please have a look at the following code, which uses a JavaScript variable inside JSX:

```
function App() {
  const userName = 'Some Name';
  return (
    <div>
      <p>Hello {userName}!</p>
    </div>
  )
}
```

In this example, we are greeting a user whose name we have previously stored in a `userName` variable by inserting this `userName` variable into our example code's JSX.

These JSX tags are really handy, but what if I have some part of the code that I want to reuse throughout the code, such as a special kind of button or a sidebar element? This is where the *component-based* catchphrase from the ReactJS home page comes into play.

Understanding React components

Our example includes one component called App. In this case, it's a functional component. It's also possible to use class components in React but most of the following examples will use the more common functional components. React allows you to write custom components and use them exactly like a normal JSX tag in another part of the code.

Let's say we want to have a button that opens an external link to the ReactJS home page upon being clicked. We could define a custom `ReactButton` component like this:

```
function ReactButton() {
  const link = 'https://reactjs.org';
  return (
    <div>
      <a href={link} target="_blank" rel="noopener noreferrer">
        Go To React
      </a>
    </div>
  )
}
```

Then, we can use the button in the main component, using the empty tag notation as it doesn't have any child components:

```
function App() {
  const userName = 'Some Name';
  return (
    <div>
      <p>Hello {userName}!</p>
      <ReactButton/>
    </div>
  )
}
```

As you can see, every component in React has to implement the `return` function to render a view in the app. The JSX code can only be executed when it is called by the `return` function, and there has to be one JSX tag that wraps all the other tags and components. There is no need to explicitly implement how the view should behave when the content changes – React automatically handles this. This is what we mean when we describe React as being declarative.

So far, we have seen why React is defined as a declarative, component-based JavaScript library for building user interfaces. But we haven't talked about one of the main advantages of React yet: how it efficiently rerenders views. To understand this, we need to have a look at props and state.

Understanding React props and state

A **prop** is a parameter that is transferred from a parent component to a child component. Let's say we want to create a `WelcomeMessage` component that shows a welcoming text, including the username from the `App` component.

This component could look like this:

```
function WelcomeMessage(props) {
  return (
    <div>
      <p>Welcome {props.userName}!</p>
      <p>It's nice to see you here!</p>
    </div>
  )
}
```

Then, we can include it in the `App` component:

```
function App() {
  const userName = "Some Name";
  return (
    <div>
      <WelcomeMessage userName={userName}/>
      <ReactButton/>
    </div>
  )
}
```

The name of the prop is used like an attribute on the JSX tag of the child component. By using `props` as a parameter for the child component, all those attributes are automatically accessible in the child component, such as `username` in our example.

What makes React so efficient is the fact that any time the value of a prop changes, only those components that are affected by that change are rerendered. This massively reduces the rerendering costs, especially for large applications with many layers.

The same goes for state changes. React provides the possibility to turn any component into a stateful component by implementing the `state` variable in class components or the `useState` Hook (more on Hooks in *Chapter 3, Hello React Native*) in functional components. The classical example of a stateful component is a `Counter`:

```
function Counter () {
  const [numClicks, setNumClicks] = useState(0);
  return (
    <div>
      <p>You have clicked {numClicks} times!</>
      <button onClick={() => setNumClicks(numClicks+1)>
        Click Me
      </button>
    </div>
  )
}
```

The `numClicks` state variable is initialized with a value of 0. Any time the user clicks on the button and the internal state of the `Counter` component changes, only the content of the `<p>` tag is rerendered.

ReactDOM is responsible for comparing all the elements in the UI tree with the previous ones and updating only the nodes whose content has changed. This package also makes it possible to easily integrate React code into existing web apps, regardless of what language they are written in.

When Facebook decided to become a mobile-first company in 2012, this *learn once, write anywhere* approach of React was applied to the development of mobile applications, which led to the emergence of React Native in 2013, where it is possible to write apps for iOS or Android using only JavaScript or TypeScript.

Now that we have learned what React is and how it works in general, let's learn more about React Native.

Introducing React Native

React Native is a framework that makes it possible to write React code and deploy it to multiple platforms. The most well known are iOS and Android, but you can use React Native to create apps for

Windows, macOS, Oculus, Linux, tvOS, and much more. With React Native for Web, you can even deploy a mobile application as a web app using the same code.

> **Tip**
>
> If you don't want to spend an hour setting up the development environment for creating a new React Native app and trying out the code examples, you could install the Expo CLI using npm or yarn:
>
> **npm install -g expo-cli   OR   yarn global add expo-cli**
>
> After that, setting up a new React Native app just takes running one command in the terminal:
>
> **expo init NameOfYourApp**
>
> **Pro tip**: The default package manager for a new app created by running expo init is yarn. If you want to use npm instead, add --npm to the expo init command.

In the next section, you will learn how cross-platform development is made possible in the React Native framework.

React Native basics

As React Native is heavily based on React, the code looks much the same; you use components to structure the code, props to hand over parameters from one component to another, and JSX in a return statement to render the view. One of the main differences is the type of basic JSX components you can use.

In React, they look a lot like XML/HTML tags, as we have seen in the previous section. In React Native, the so-called core components are imported from the react-native library and look different:

```
import React from 'react';
import {ScrollView, Text, View} from 'react-native';


const App = () => {
  return (
    <ScrollView contentInsetAdjustmentBehavior="automatic">
        <View>
            <Text>Hello World!</Text>
        </View>
    </ScrollView>
  );
};


export default App;
```

React Native does not use web views to render the JavaScript code on the device like some other cross-platform solutions; instead, it converts the UI written in JavaScript into native UI elements. The React Native `View` component, for example, gets converted into a `ViewGroup` component for Android, and into a `UIView` component for iOS. This conversion is done via the Yoga engine (`https://yogalayout.com`).

React Native is powered by two threads – the JavaScript thread, where the JavaScript code is executed, and the native thread (or UI thread), where all device interaction such as user input and drawing screens happens.

The communication between these two threads takes place over the so-called **Bridge**, which is a kind of interface between the JavaScript code and the native part of the app. Information such as native events or instructions is sent in serialized batches from the native UI thread over the Bridge to the JavaScript thread and back. This process is shown in the following diagram:

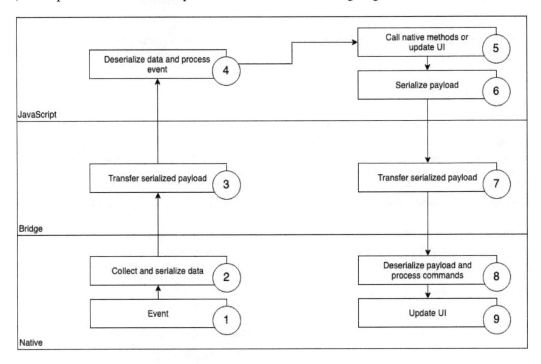

Figure 1.1 – React Native Bridge

As you can see, events are collected in the native thread. The information is then serialized and passed to the JavaScript thread via the Bridge. In the JavaScript thread, information is deserialized and processed. This also works the other way round, as you can see in *Steps 5* to *8* of the preceding diagram. You can call methods, which are provided by native components, or React Native can update the UI when necessary. This is also done by serializing the information and passing it to the native thread via the Bridge. This Bridge makes it possible to communicate between native and JavaScript in an asynchronous way, which is great to create real native apps with JavaScript.

But it also has some downsides. The serialization and deserialization of information, as well as being the only central point of communication between native and JS, makes the bridge a bottleneck that can cause performance issues in some situations. This is why React Native was completely rewritten between 2018 and 2022.

The new React Native (2022)

Because of the architectural problems mentioned previously, the React Native core was rearchitectured and rewritten completely. The main goal was to get rid of the Bridge and the performance issues tied to it. This was done by introducing JSI, the JavaScript interface, which allows direct communication between native and JavaScript code without the need for serialization/deserialization.

The JS part is truly aware of the native objects, which means you can directly call methods synchronously. Also, a new renderer was introduced during the rearchitecture, which is called Fabric. More details on the React Native rearchitecture will be provided in *Chapter 3, Hello React Native*.

The rearchitecture made the awesome React Native framework even more awesome by improving its out-of-the-box performance significantly. At the time of writing, more and more packages are being adapted to the new React Native architecture.

More React Native advantages

Ever since it was open-sourced in 2015, there has been a huge and ever-growing community that develops and provides a lot of add-on packages for a multitude of different problems and use cases. This is one of the main advantages that React Native has over other, similar cross-platform approaches.

These packages are mostly well maintained and provide nearly all native functionality that currently exists, so you only have to work with JavaScript to write your apps.

This means using React Native for mobile app development makes it possible to reduce the size of the developer team greatly, as you no longer need both Android and iOS specialists, or you can at least reduce the team size of native specialists significantly.

And the best thing about working with these well-maintained packages is that things such as the React Native core rewrites come to your app automatically when the packages are updated.

Additionally, the hot reload feature speeds up the development process by making it possible to see the effect of code changes in a matter of seconds. Several other tools make the life of a React Native developer even more comfortable, which we will look at in more detail in *Chapter 9, Essential Tools for Improving React Native Development*.

Now that we understand what React and React Native are, and how they are related to each other, let's have a look at a tool that makes the whole development process much easier – Expo.

Introducing Expo

There are several ways to set up a new React Native app. For the example project in this book, we will use Expo. It's a powerful framework built on top of React Native that includes many different tools and libraries. Expo uses plain React Native and enhances it with a lot of functionality.

While React Native is a very lean framework when it comes to core components and native functionality, Expo provides nearly every functionality that you can think of using in your app. It provides components and APIs for nearly all native device functions, such as video playback, sensors, location, security, device information, and a lot more.

Think of Expo as a full-service package that makes your life as a React Native developer a lot easier. Since everything comes with a downside, Expo adds some size to your final app bundle, because you add all the libraries to your app whether you use them or not.

It also uses a somehow modified version of React Native, which is normally one or two versions behind the latest React Native version. So, when working with Expo, you have to wait for the latest React Native features a couple of months after they are released.

I would recommend using Expo if you want to achieve results at maximum speed and don't have to optimize your bundle size.

When setting up a new project with Expo, you can choose between two different types of workflows – a bare workflow and a managed workflow. In both workflows, the framework provides you with easy-to-use libraries for including native elements such as the camera, the filesystem, and others. Additionally, services such as push notification handling, over-the-air feature updates, and a special Expo build service for iOS and Android builds are available.

If you choose the bare workflow, you have a plain React Native app and can add the Expo libraries you need. You can also add other third-party libraries, which is not possible in the managed workflow. There, you only write JavaScript or TypeScript code in the IDE of your choice; everything else is handled by the framework.

On their home page (`https://docs.expo.dev/`), Expo suggests that you start with a managed workflow for a new app because it is always possible to switch over to a bare workflow, if necessary, by using the `expo eject` command in the CLI. This necessity can arise if you need to integrate a third-party package or library that is not supported by Expo, or if you want to add or change native code.

After initializing the app, you can run it by using the `expo start` command. This will start up the Metro bundler, which compiles the JavaScript code of the app using Babel. Additionally, it opens the Expo Developer CLI interface, where you can choose which simulator you want to open the app in, as shown in the following screenshot:

```
● ● ●          🖥 my-app — node ‹ node ~/.nvm/versions/node/v14.18.2/bin/yarn start — 103×31
Starting project at /Users/alexanderkuttig/Documents/professional-rn-code/my-app
Starting Metro Bundler
```

```
› Metro waiting on exp://192.168.2.182:19000
› Scan the QR code above with Expo Go (Android) or the Camera app (iOS)

› Press a │ open Android
› Press i │ open iOS simulator
› Press w │ open web

› Press r │ reload app
› Press m │ toggle menu

› Press ? │ show all commands

Logs for your project will appear below. Press Ctrl+C to exit.
```

Figure 1.2 – Expo CLI Interface

Expo Developer Tools provides access to the Metro bundler logs. It also creates key bindings for multiple options regarding how to run the app, such as iOS or Android simulators. Finally it creates a QR code that can be scanned with the Expo Go app. Expo even supports creating web applications from React Native code for most use cases.

With Expo, it's very easy to run your app on a hard device – just install the Expo app on your smartphone or tablet and scan the QR code, as described previously. It's also possible to run the app on several devices or simulators at the same time.

All these features make Expo a very handy and easy-to-use framework for mobile app development with React Native.

Summary

In this chapter, we introduced the main concepts of the JavaScript library React. We have shown that React is declarative, component-based, and follows a *learn once, write everywhere* approach. These concepts are the base for the cross-platform mobile development framework React Native.

You saw the main advantages of this framework, namely the huge community that provides additional packages and libraries, the fact that a lot of operating systems besides iOS and Android are available, and the usage of native elements via the Bridge or JSI. Last but not least, you discovered Expo as one way of setting up a React Native app, and you know when to use which Expo workflow.

In the next chapter, we will briefly talk about the most important facts and features of JavaScript and TypeScript.

2

Understanding the Essentials of JavaScript and TypeScript

Since React Native apps are written in JavaScript, it is important to have a very good understanding of this language to build high-quality apps. JavaScript is very easy to learn, but very hard to master, because it allows you to do nearly everything without giving you a hard time. However, just because you can do everything does not mean that you should.

The overall goal of this chapter is to show important underlying concepts for avoiding the most common mistakes, bad patterns, and very expensive *don'ts*. You will get useful tips, learn best practices, and repeat the most important basics to use JavaScript in your apps.

In this chapter, we will cover the following topics:

- Exploring modern JavaScript
- JavaScript knowledge for React Native development
- Working with asynchronous JavaScript
- Using typed JavaScript

Technical requirements

There are no technical requirements except a browser to run the examples of this chapter. Just go to `https://jsfiddle.com/` or `https://codesandbox.io/` and type and run your code.

To access the code for this chapter, follow this link to the book's GitHub repository:

This chapter is not a complete tutorial. If you are not familiar with the JavaScript basics, please have a look at `https://javascript.info`, which is the JavaScript tutorial I would recommend to start.

Exploring modern JavaScript

When we speak of modern **JavaScript**, this refers to ECMAScript 2015 (which also is known as ES6) or newer. It contains a lot of useful features, which are not included in older JavaScript versions. Since 2015 there has been an update to the specification released every year.

You can have a look at the features that were implemented in previous releases in the TC39 GitHub repository (`https://bit.ly/prn-js-proposals`). You can also find a lot of information about upcoming features and release plans there.

Let's start our journey to understand the most important parts of JavaScript by having a look under the hood. To truly understand modern JavaScript and the tooling around it, we have to take a little look at the basics and the history of the language. JavaScript is a script language, which can run nearly everywhere.

The most common use case clearly is building dynamic frontends for the web browser, but it also runs on the server (Node.js), as part of other software, on microcontrollers, or (most importantly for us) in apps.

Every place where JavaScript runs has to have a JavaScript engine, which is responsible for executing the JavaScript code. In older browsers, the engines were only simple interpreters that transformed the code to executable bytecode at runtime without any optimizations.

Today there is a lot of optimization going on inside the different JS engines, depending on which metrics are important for the engine's use case. The Chromium V8 engine, for example, introduced just-in-time compilation, which resulted in a huge performance boost while executing JavaScript.

To be able to have a common understanding of what JavaScript is on all those platforms and between all those engines, JavaScript has a standardized specification called ES. This specification is constantly evolving as more and more features (such as improved asynchrony or a cleaner syntax) are introduced to JavaScript.

This constantly evolving feature set is awesome for developers but introduced a big problem. To be able to use the new features of the ES language specification, the JavaScript engine in question has to implement the new features and then the new version of the engine has to be rolled out to all users.

This is a big problem especially when it comes to browsers, since a lot of companies rely on very old browsers for their infrastructure. This would make it impossible for developers to use the new features for years.

This is where transcompilers such as Babel (`https://babeljs.io`) come into play. These transcompilers convert modern JavaScript into a backward-compatible version, which can be executed by older JavaScript engines. This transcompilation is an important step of the build process in modern web applications as well as in React Native apps.

When writing modern JavaScript applications, it works like this:

1. You write your code in modern JavaScript.

2. A transcompiler converts your code to pre-ES6 JavaScript.

3. A JavaScript engine interprets your code and transforms it into bytecode, which is then executed on the machine.

4. Modern JavaScript engines optimize execution with features such as just-in-time compilation.

When it comes to React Native, you can choose from different JavaScript engines with different strengths and weaknesses. You can read more on this in *Chapter 8, JavaScript Engines and Hermes*.

In this section, you learned what modern JavaScript is and how it works under the hood. Let's continue with the specific parts of JavaScript required when developing with React Native.

Exploring JavaScript for React Native development

In this section, you will learn some basic JavaScript concepts, all of which are important to truly understand how to work with React Native. Again, this is not a complete tutorial; it includes only the most important things that you have to keep in mind if you don't want to run into errors that are very hard to debug.

> Tip
>
> When you are not sure how JavaScript behaves in a special scenario, just create an isolated example and try it on `https://jsfiddle.com/` or `https://codesandbox.io/`.

Understanding the assigning and passing of objects

Assigning or passing data is one of the most basic operations in any programming language. You do it a lot in every project. When working with JavaScript, there is a difference when working with primitive types (Boolean, number, string, and so on) or with objects (or arrays, which are basically objects).

Primitives are assigned and passed by values, while objects are assigned and passed by references. This means for primitives, a real copy of the value is created and stored, while for objects, only a new reference to the same object is created and stored.

This is important to keep in mind, because when you edit an assigned or passed object, you also edit the initial object.

This will be clearer in the following code example:

```javascript
function paintRed(vehicle) {
    vehicle.color = ' red >;
}


const bus = {
    color: 'blue'
}
paintRed(bus);
console.log(bus.color); // red
```

The `paintRed` function does not return anything and we do not write anything in `bus` after initializing it as a blue bus. So, what happens? The `bus` object is passed as a reference. This means the `vehicle` variable in the `paintRed` function and the `bus` variable outside of the function reference the same object in storage.

When changing the color of `vehicle`, we change the color of the object that is also referenced by `bus`.

This is expected behavior, but you should avoid using it in most cases. In larger projects, code can get very hard to read (and debug) when objects are passed down a lot of functions and are then changed. As Robert C. Martin already wrote in the book *Clean Code*, functions should have no side effects, which means they should not change values outside of the function's scope.

If you want to change an object in a function, I recommend using a return value in most cases. This is much easier to understand and read. The following example shows the code from the previous example, but without side effects:

```javascript
function paintRed(vehicle) {
const _vehicle = { ...vehicle }

    _vehicle.color = 'red'

return _vehicle;
}
let bus = {
    color: 'blue'
}

bus = paintRed(bus);
console.log(bus.color); // red
```

In this code example, it is absolutely clear that bus is a new object, which was created by the paintRed function.

Please keep this in mind when working on your projects. It really can cost you a lot of time when you have to debug a change in your object, but you don't know where it's coming from.

Creating real copies of an object

A very common problem that results from the previous point is that you have to clone an object. There are multiple ways to do that, each with different limitations. Three options are shown in the following code example:

```
const car = {

color: 'red',
        extras: {
            radio: "premium",
            ac: false
        },
        sellingDate: new Date(),
        writeColor: function() {
            console.log('This car is ' + this.color);
}
};

const _car = {...car};
const _car2 = Object.assign({}, car);
const _car3 = JSON.parse(JSON.stringify(car));

car.extras.ac = true;

console.log(_car);
console.log(_car2);
console.log(_car3);
```

We create an object with different types as properties. This is important, because the different ways to clone the object will not work for all properties. We use a string for color, an object for extras, a date for sellingDate, and a function in writeColor to return a string with the color of the car.

In the next lines, we use three different ways to clone the object. After creating the `_car`, `_car2`, and `_car3` cloned objects, we change `extras` in the initial `car` object. We then log all three objects.

We will now have a detailed look at the different options regarding how to clone objects in JavaScript. These are the following:

- Spread operator and `Object.assign`
- `JSON.stringify` and `JSON.parse`
- Real deepclone

We'll start with spread operator and `Object.assign`, which basically work the same way.

Spread operator and Object.assign

The three dots we use to create `_car` is called a **spread operator**. It returns all properties of the object. So basically, in line 13 we created a new object and populated it with all properties of `car`. In line 14, we did a very similar thing; we assigned all properties of `car` to a new empty object with `Object.assign`.

In fact, lines 13 and 14 work the same way. They create a **shallow clone**, which means they clone all property values of the object.

This works great for values, but it doesn't for complex data types, because, again, objects are assigned by reference. So, these ways of creating a copy of a complex object only clone the references to the data of the properties of the object and don't create real copies of every property.

In our example, we wouldn't create a real copy of `extras`, `sellingDate`, and `writeColor`, because the values of the properties in the `car` object are only references to the objects. This means that by changing `_car.extras` in line 17, we also change `_car2.extras`, because it references the same object.

So these ways of cloning objects work fine for objects with just one level. As soon as there is an object with multiple levels, cloning with the spread operator or `Object.assign` can create serious problems in your application.

Stringify and parse again

A very common pattern to clone objects is to use the built-in `JSON.stringify` and `JSON.parse` features of JavaScript. This converts the object to a primitive type (a JSON string) and creates a new object by parsing the string again.

This forces a **deepclone**, which means even sub-objects are copied by value. The downside of this approach is that it only works for values that have an equivalent in JSON.

So, you will lose all functions, properties that are undefined, and values such as infinity that do not exist in JSON. Other things such as date objects will be simplified as strings, resulting in a lost time zone. So, this solution works great for deep objects with primitive values.

Real deepclone

When you want to create a real deepclone of an object, you have to get creative and write your own function. There are a lot of different approaches when you search the web. I would recommend using a well-tested and maintained library such as Lodash (`https://lodash.com/`). It offers a simple `cloneDeep` function, which does the work for you.

You can use all solutions, but you have to keep in mind the limitations of every single approach. You should also have a look at the performance of the different solutions when you use them. In most cases, all cloning methods are fast enough to use, but when you're experiencing performance issues in your application, you should have a closer look at which method you are using.

Please find a summary in the following table:

	Spread Operator / Object.assign	JSON.parse JSON.stringify	Real Deepclone (Lodash cloneDeep)
Clone first-level primitives	Yes	Yes	Yes
Clone second–nth level primitives	No	Yes	Yes
Clone date properties	Only reference	Only string value	Yes
Clone function properties	Only reference	No	Yes
Performance	Fast	Slow	Medium

Figure 2.1 – Comparison of JavaScript cloning solutions

Knowing how to clone objects in certain situations is very important, because using the wrong cloning technique can lead to errors that are very hard to debug.

After understanding how to clone objects, let's have a look at destructuring objects.

Working with destructuring in JavaScript

Another thing you will need to do a lot when working with React Native is destructuring objects and arrays. Destructuring basically means *unpacking* the properties of objects or the elements of arrays. Especially when working with Hooks, this is something you have to know very well. Let's start with arrays.

Destructuring arrays

Have a look at the following code example, which shows how an array gets destructured:

```
let name = ["John", "Doe"];
let [firstName, lastName] = name;
console.log(firstName); // John
console.log(lastName); // Doe
```

You can see an array with two elements. In the second line, we *destructure* the name array by assigning name to an array with two variables inside. The first variable gets assigned the first value of the array, and the second variable the second value. This can also be done with more than two values.

Array destructuring is used, for example, every time you work with a useState Hook (more on this in *Chapter 3, Hello React Native*).

Now that you know how to destructure an array, let's go on to destructuring objects.

Destructuring objects

The following code example shows how to destructure an object:

```
let person = {
    firstName: "John",
    lastName: "Doe",
    age: 33
}
let {firstName, age} = person;
console.log(firstName); // John
console.log(age); // 33
```

Object destructuring works the same way as destructuring arrays. But please note the curly brackets in line 6 of the code example. This is important when destructuring objects instead of arrays. You *can* get all properties of the object just by using the key in the destructuring, but you don't have to use all properties. In our example, we only use firstName and age, but not lastName.

When working with destructuring, you can also collect all the elements that weren't specified during the destructuring. This is done with the spread operator, as described in the following section.

Using the spread operator during destructuring

The spread operator can be used as shown in the following code example:

```
const person = {
      firstName: '      n',
      lastName: 'Doe',
      age: 33,
      height: 176
}
const {firstName, age, ...rest} = person;
console.log(firstName); // John
console.log(age); // 33


console.log(Object.keys(rest).length); // 2
```

When destructuring arrays or objects, you can use the spread operator to collect all elements that weren't included in the destructuring. In the code example, we use `firstName` and `age` in the destructuring.

All other properties, in this example `lastName` and `height`, are collected in a new object, the `rest` variable. This is used a lot in React and React Native, for example when passing properties (or props) down to components and destructuring these props.

When you work with React or React Native, especially with functional components and Hooks, destructuring is something that you will use in every component. Basically, it is nothing more than *unpacking* the properties of an object or elements of an array.

Now that we understand destructuring, let's move on to another important topic – the `this` keyword and its scope in JavaScript.

Understanding this in JavaScript

JavaScript has quite a unique behavior when it comes to the `this` keyword. It does not always refer to the function or scope where it is used. By default, `this` is bound to the global scope. This can be changed via implicit or explicit binding.

Implicit and explicit binding

Implicit binding means that if a function is called as part of an object, `this` always refers to the object. **Explicit binding** means that you can bind `this` to another context. This is something that was used a lot in React and React Native to bind `this` in the handlers of class components.

Please have a look at the following code example:

```
class MyClass extends Component{
        constructor( props ){
                this.handlePress =
                    this.handlePress.bind(this);
        }
handlePress(event){
                console.log(this);
        }
render(){
                return (
                    <Pressable type="button"
                        onPress={this.handlePress}>
                        <Text>Button</Text>
                    </Pressable >
                );
        }
}
```

In the preceding code, we bind the `this` value of the class explicitly to the `handlePress` function. This is necessary, because if we don't do it, `this` would be implicitly bound to the object where it is called, which in this case would be anywhere in the `Pressable` component. Since we want to have access to the data of our `MyClass` component in our `handlePress` function in most cases, this explicit binding is needed.

You can see this kind of code in a lot of applications, because for a long time it was the only method to access class properties from inside a function. This led to a lot of explicit binding statements in constructors, especially in larger class components. Fortunately, today there is a much better solution – arrow functions!

Arrow functions to the rescue

In modern JavaScript, there is another solution that makes this implicit/explicit binding redundant: **arrow functions**. This is a new syntax to define functions, which is not only shorter than the old way of declaring functions, but it also changes the way that the value of the this keyword is bound. Instead of writing function myFunction(param1){}, you simply write const myFunction = (param1) => {}.

The important thing here is that arrow functions always use the lexical scope of this, which means they won't rebind this implicitly.

The following example shows how to use arrow functions to make explicit binding statements redundant:

```
class MyClass extends Component{
handlePress = (event) => {
            console.log(this);
        }
render(){
            return (
                <Pressable type="button"
                    onPress={this.handlePress}>
                    <Text>Button</Text>
                </Pressable >
            );
        }
}
```

As you can see, we use an arrow function to define handlePress. Because of this, we don't have to do an explicit binding like in the code example before. We simply can use this inside the handlePress function to access states and props of other properties of our MyClass component. This makes the code easier to write, read, and maintain.

> **Important note**
> Please keep in mind that regular functions and arrow functions are not only syntactically different, but they also change the way this is bound.

Understanding the scope of this is crucial to avoid costly errors such as undefined object references. When it comes to app development, these undefined object references can hard-crash your app. So, keep in mind the scope you are referring to when using the this keyword.

These are the most important things you must truly understand when using JavaScript to develop large-scale applications. If you don't, you will make costly errors.

The next thing that is very important when developing apps with React Native is asynchronous programming.

Working with asynchronous JavaScript

Because of the architecture of React Native (more on this in *Chapter 3, Hello React Native*) and the typical use cases of apps, understanding asynchronous JavaScript is crucial. A typical example of an asynchronous call is a call to an API.

In a synchronous world, after making the call, the application would be blocked until the answer from the API is received. This is, obviously, unexpected behavior. The application should respond to user interaction while it waits for the response. This means the call to the API has to be done asynchronously.

There are multiple ways of working with asynchronous calls in JavaScript. The first one is callbacks.

Exploring callbacks

Callbacks are the most basic way to work with asynchrony in JavaScript. I would recommend using them as little as possible, because there are better alternatives. But since a lot of libraries rely on callbacks, you have to have a good understanding of them.

A callback is a JavaScript function A that is passed as an argument to another function B. At some point in function B, function A is called. This behavior is called a **callback**. The following code shows a simple callback example:

```
const A = (callback) => {
    console.log("function A called");
    callback();
}
const B = () => {
    console.log("function B called");
}
A(B);
// function A called
// function B called
```

When you look at the code, function A is called. It logs some text and then calls the callback. This callback is the function passed to function A as a property when function A was called – in this example, function B.

So, function B is called at the end of function A. Function B then logs some more text. As a result of this code, you will see two lines of text: first, the one logged by function A, and second, the one logged by function B.

While callbacks can be a little hard to understand, let's have a look at what's happening under the hood.

Understanding the implementation

To be able to truly understand callbacks, we'll have to dig a little into the implementation of a JavaScript engine. JavaScript is single-threaded, so inside of the JavaScript code execution, asynchrony won't be possible. The following figure shows the important parts of a JavaScript engine and how they work together to achieve asynchrony:

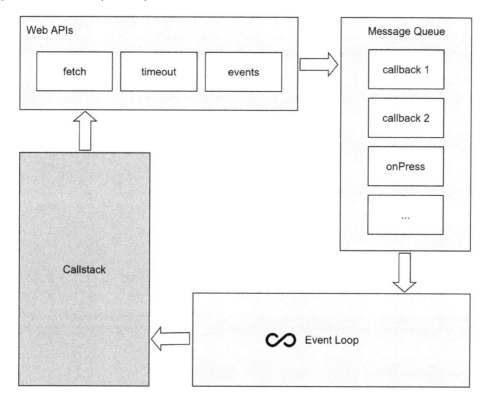

Figure 2.2 – JavaScript engine asynchronous code execution

Your commands will be pushed to the **callstack** and processed in a last-in, first-out order. To achieve asynchrony, JavaScript engines provide APIs that are called from within your JavaScript code. These APIs execute code on another thread. Most of these APIs expect a callback passed as an argument.

When this code execution on the second thread is finished, this callback will be pushed to the **message queue**. The message queue is monitored by the **event loop**. As soon as the callstack is empty and the message queue is not, the event loop takes the first item of the message queue and pushes it on the callstack. Now we are back in our JavaScript context and the JavaScript code execution continues with the given callback.

What's better than callbacks? Promises!

With ES 2015, promises were introduced. Under the hood, they work quite similar to callbacks, except that there is another queue called a job or microtask queue. This queue works like the message queue but has a higher priority when getting processed by the event loop.

The difference from callbacks is that promises have a much cleaner syntax. While you can pass any number of callbacks to a function, a promise returns a function with exactly one or two arguments – resolve and (optionally) reject. resolve is called when the promise is processed successfully, and reject if there was an error while processing the promise.

The following code shows a generic example of a promise and how it is used:

```
const myPromise = () => new Promise((resolve) => {
    setTimeout(() => {
        resolve();
        }, 500);

});
console.log('start promise');
myPromise()
.then(() => {
    console.log('promise resolved');
});
// start promise
// -- 500ms delay


// promise resolved
```

The promise is created with new Promise and then called. Inside the promise, there is a 500 ms delay before the promise is resolved. When the promise is resolved, the function inside .then is called.

One of the simplest examples of this asynchronous behavior using a promise is fetching data from a server. You can use the Fetch API in JavaScript. This API contacts the server and waits for an answer.

As soon as the answer is received, resolve or reject is pushed to the queue and processed by the event loop. The following example shows the code for a simple fetch:

```
fetch("https://fakerapi.it/api/v1/texts?_quantity=1")
    .then(response => response.json())
    .then(data => {
        console.log(data);
    })
```

```
    .catch(error => {
        console.log(error); // handle or report the error
    })
```

This code example even contains two promises:

- The `fetch` operation, which returns the server response
- The unwrapping of the JSON data, which is included in the response

If one of the promises is rejected, the `catch` block is called with some error information.

> **Tip**
>
> You should always catch your errors and promise rejections and handle – or at least report – them. While unhandled promise rejections don't crash your application in most cases, it indicates that something went wrong. It can be very hard to realize and debug this error without proper error reporting in place. It is always a good idea to use reporting tools such as Sentry or Bugsnag. You can read more on this in *Chapter 14, Tips, Tricks, and Best Practices*.

Promises also provide some interesting features such as `Promises.all` and `Promises.first`, which make it possible to work with multiple promises. If you want to learn more about this, you can have a look at `bit.ly/prn-promises`.

Improved syntax with async/await

With ES 2017, the `async` and `await` keywords were introduced to work with Promises. This is the syntax I recommend you use in your projects because it makes the code easy to read and understand. Instead of chaining `.then` with a callback function to the promise call, you can simply `await` the promise.

The only requirement is that the function you write code in is declared as an async function. You can also wrap the call with a `try/catch` block. This is similar to `.catch` in the regular promise syntax. The following example shows how to work with `async/await` property:

```
const fetchData = async () => {
try {
const response = await fetch(
"https://fakerapi.it/api/v1/texts?_quantity=1");
const data = await response.json();
console.log(data);
} catch (error) {
        console.log(error);
```

```
        }
    }
    fetchData();
```

We specify `fetchData` as an `async` function with the `async` keyword. Inside the async function, we use `try/catch` for proper error handling. Inside the `try` block, we await the `fetch` call and the unpacking of the JSON body with the `await` keyword.

Basically, every promise can be used with the async/await syntax. Also, an async function can be handled as a Promise with `.then` and `.catch`. Again, this is the syntax I would recommend for use in large-scale projects. Since it is compatible with Promises, you can use a lot of libraries with it out of the box. But when you have to work with a library that relies on promises in its API, you will have to patch it.

Patching callback libraries

When working with React Native, you will find some libraries that work with callbacks in their JavaScript. This is because the transfer between the JavaScript and React Native contexts relies on callbacks in most cases. I would recommend patching these libraries and reworking them to provide a promise API, which you can then use with async/await in your project. This is quite simple and improves the code quality a lot. A very simple example is shown in the following code block:

```
// libraryFunction(successCallback, errorCallback);
const libraryFunctionPromise = new Promise((resolve, reject) =>
{
    libraryFunction(resolve, reject);
}
```

In this code example, we have a library that provides a function that expects a `successCallback` and an `errorCallback`. We create a promise, which just calls this function and passes `resolve` as `successCallback` and `reject` as `errorCallback`. That's all, now we can work with async/await to call our promise, which then calls the library function for us.

> **Tip**
> Try to use async/await syntax over promises wherever possible. This makes your code easier to read and understand.

In this section, you learned how asynchrony is implemented in JavaScript, how callbacks and promises work, and why you should rely on async/await, especially in large-scale projects.

This leads to the last section of this chapter, which is also very important when working on large-scale projects – static type checking in JavaScript.

Using typed JavaScript

JavaScript is a dynamically typed language. This means you can change the type of a variable after its initialization. While this can be very handy for small scripts, it can lead to difficult problems when working on large-scale projects. Debugging such errors, especially in apps with a lot of users, can get really messy.

This is where extensions to JavaScript come into play. There are multiple solutions to extend JavaScript to be a typed language. This not only prevents errors; it also enables better refactoring and code completion as well as pointing out problems directly when writing the code.

This speeds up the development process a lot. I would definitely recommend using typed JavaScript and I want to introduce the two most popular solutions here.

Flow

Created and open sourced by Facebook, Flow is a static type checker that works with normal JavaScript. It was created as a command-line tool that scans your files for type safety and reports errors to the console. Nowadays, all common JavaScript IDEs have Flow support built in or offer it via excellent plugins.

To enable static type checking with Flow, you just have to add the `// @flow` annotation to the top of your file. This tells the Flow type checker to include the file in the check. Then you can directly add your types behind the declaration of variables and parameters (inline), or you can declare more complex types and use these types to specify the type of a variable when it is declared.

This is shown in the following code block:

```
type Person = {
    name: string,
    height: number,
    age: number
}
let john: Person = {
    name: "John",
    height: 180,
    age: 35
}
```

We created a `Person` type, which is then used to create a person, `john`. If we had missed one of the properties or had assigned a value with the wrong type, the Flow IDE integration would have given us an error.

Since Flow isn't a separate language but only a tool on top of JavaScript, we have to transform our files from Flow annotated files back to *normal* JavaScript files. This basically means, we have to use a transformer to remove all the Flow annotations from our files. Flow provides a Babel plugin for this, which has to be installed for your project to work.

Flow can be configured via a `.flowconfig` file. Here you can define which files and folders should be checked and which shouldn't, as well as specifying some options, such as how to deal with imports, but also how many workers Flow can start in parallel to check your code or how much memory Flow is allowed to use.

If you want to have a deeper look at Flow, please visit the website at `https://flow.org/`.

TypeScript

Another option for typed JavaScript is TypeScript. It is an open source language on top of JavaScript that is developed and maintained by Microsoft. It also has awesome integrations for all common JavaScript IDEs and works very similar to Flow.

Your TypeScript code will be transformed into plain JavaScript via the TypeScript transpiler or Babel, before you are able to execute it in production. Even the syntax of the annotations is nearly the same. The example code in the *Flow* section would work perfectly fine in TypeScript.

If you want to have a deeper look at TypeScript, please visit the website at `www.typescriptlang.org`.

In general, I prefer TypeScript over Flow, because it is used much more widely with much larger support from the community. The docs are better and so are the IDE integration and code completion. If you start a new project, I recommend going with TypeScript. But Flow is also a good solution. If you have a working Flow integration in your project, there is no need to migrate to TypeScript at the moment.

> **Important note**
> If you work on a large-scale project, I would definitely recommend using Flow or TypeScript. Even if you have some overhead at the beginning, it will save you much more time and money in the end.

Summary

In this chapter, we learned how modern JavaScript works, along with some especially important basics for when working with React Native, and how asynchrony works in JavaScript. You have acquired a basic understanding of the underlying technology, as well as how misuse can lead to costly errors and how to avoid them.

In the next chapter, we will learn about React, how it works internally, and which parts of React it is important to know well when working with React Native.

3
Hello React Native

After you learned the basics of React and React Native in *Chapter 1, What Is React Native?*, and the fundamentals of JavaScript and TypeScript in *Chapter 2, Understanding the Essentials of JavaScript and TypeScript*, it is now time to dive deeper into the React Native world.

One of the best things about React Native is that it is very flexible when it comes to how you use it. You can choose **Expo**, which handles all the native part for you and allows you to complete your first app in hours. It also makes it possible to build iOS apps without having a Mac. But you also can go with a bare React Native workflow, which gives you a lot of options in terms of how you integrate your React Native app into your whole development landscape.

You can also integrate or even write your own (native) libraries. While this flexibility is one of the biggest strengths of React Native, it needs you to really understand what's going on in the different scenarios to make the right choice for your project and your company.

This chapter will enable you to do so. You will truly understand the different approaches, how to leverage them, and when to use each approach.

You will learn the following things in the sections of this chapter:

- Understanding how React Native works on an example app
- Passing properties
- Understanding class components, function components, and Hooks
- Connecting different platforms to JavaScript
- Introducing the new React Native Architecture

Technical requirements

To be able to run the code in this chapter, you have to set up the following things:

- A working React Native environment (`https://reactnative.dev/docs/environment-setup`—**React Native command-line interface (CLI)** quickstart guide)
- While most of this chapter should also work on Windows, I would recommend working on a Mac

Understanding how React Native works on an example app

There is no better way to understand a technology than by working with it. This section contains a simple example app that will show information about movies based on a static **JavaScript Object Notation (JSON)** file. The app will be further developed in the next chapters. For now, it should contain the following views:

- A home view to show a list of movie categories
- A category detail page with information about the category as well as the most popular movies of the category, with title and poster
- A movie detail page with information about the movie, including title, poster, rating, release date, and description

While this is a very simple example, we'll use it to focus a lot on understanding what's going on under the hood. But let's start with creating the app. We'll use a React Native bare workflow to be complete in control while not having any overhead. That means we are using the official React Native CLI to initialize our project. This is done with the following command:

```
npx react-native init videoexample
    --template react-native-template-typescript
```

We are using a TypeScript template to directly set up our project as a TypeScript project. This includes the **TypeScript compiler (tsc)** as well as the correct file extensions. You will learn more about templates and other options to start a React Native project in *Chapter 9, Essential Tools for Improving React Native Development*.

The preceding command creates a `videoexample` folder that contains the new React Native project. If you have set up everything correctly, you can start your example app on your iOS simulator with `cd videoexample && npx react-native run-ios` (iOS simulators only work on iOS; on Windows, you can use `cd videoexample && npx react-native run-android` to start an Android simulator).

When you have successfully started your simulator, you should see the React Native default app running. It should look like this:

Figure 3.1 – React Native default app

When you open the `videoexample` folder in your **integrated development environment** (IDE), you will see that the React Native CLI has created a lot of files for you. In the following subsection, you'll learn what they are and what they do.

Understanding the React Native example project

The example project has only one screen, but technically it is a complete Android and iOS app. This means it contains the following things:

- `android`: This folder contains the native Android project. You can open this folder with Android Studio and work with it like a native Android app. It uses Gradle as the build system, which also is integrated very nicely into Android Studio. The most important files you may have to touch on at some point in time are the following ones:

- `android/app/src/main/AndroidManifest.xml`: The Android manifest contains essential information about the app. You may have to edit this file when adding certain functionality to your app that needs user permission or starting the app from push notifications.

- `android/app/src/main/java/com/<youridentifier>/MainApplication.java` & `android/app/src/main/java/com/<youridentifier>/MainApplication.java`: These are the main files of your application. Normally you don't have to touch these, but some libraries need some extra configuration here to work correctly.

- `android/app/build.gradle`: This file defines the Android build process for your app. In most cases, React Native handles this automatically, even if you install third-party libraries with native parts. But in some cases, you can have conflicts between these libraries, or you have to do some additional configuration. In these cases, this is the file to look at. There is also another build file in `android/build.gradle`, where you can add configurations for all sub-projects/modules.

- `iOS`: This folder contains the native iOS project. It consists of your app project, and something called **pods**. These pods are third-party projects that get bundled in your app to provide native functionality to React Native and all third-party libraries. The following files and folders are good to know about:

  - `<youridentifier>.xcodeproj`: This is your app's project file. It contains only your project. Don't use this in Xcode because it won't work!

  - `<youridentifier>.xcworkspace`: This is the file to work with. It contains your project as well as the pods' projects. This is the file to work with in Xcode.

  - `Podfile`: In this file, you can define dependencies for other projects. These dependencies are fetched via `cocoapods`. You can think of `cocoapods` like the npm or `yarn` package for native dependencies. In most cases, all dependencies are handled automatically by React Native, but sometimes, you must adapt the dependencies (at the time of writing—for example—on an M1 Mac). If you must do so, the Podfile is the file to look at.

> **Note on cocoapods**
> `cocoapods` is a very popular dependency management tool for iOS development. Nevertheless, it is not an official tool provided by Apple but an open source solution. The cocoapods team has no information about upcoming releases of Xcode or macOS, so it can sometimes take some time for `cocoapods` to work well with the latest releases.

- `node_modules`: This folder is completely autogenerated during the dependency installation process with `npm install` or `yarn`. You don't have to change anything here unless you want to patch third-party libraries.

> **Hint on patching libraries**
>
> Sometimes, it can be useful to patch an existing library to fix a bug or add certain functionality. In these cases, you can either maintain your own fork of this library (which is very time-consuming) or you can use `patch-package`. `patch-package` is a small tool that creates patches for certain npm dependencies. You can read more on this in *Chapter 10, Structuring Large-Scale, Multi-Platform Projects.*

- `.eslintrc.js/.prettierrc.js`: A fresh React Native project comes with built-in ESLint and Prettier support. These files contain the configurations for ESLint and Prettier. For more information on these tools, please read *Chapter 9, Essential Tools for Improving React Native Development.*

- `.watchmanconfig`: React Native uses a tool called `watchman` to watch projects' files and trigger actions when they change. This is important for hot reloading during development. In most cases, this file is just an empty object.

- `app.json`: This file contains information about your app, such as the app name.

- `babel.config.js/tsconfig.json`: These files contain information, standards, and rules for the Babel and TypeScript compiler. In most cases, you don't have to edit these.

- `metro.config.js`: React Native uses a bundler called Metro to create your JavaScript bundle during development. This bundler runs on your Mac or PC, recreates your app's JavaScript bundle after you have made changes, and pushes it to your device or simulator. This file contains the configuration of the `metro` bundler. In most cases, you don't have to edit it. If you want to learn more about Metro, please visit the official page here: `https://facebook.github.io/metro/`.

- `Index.js`: This is the entry point of your JavaScript bundle. If you have a look at the code, it does nothing but bind it from `./App` to the native app via React Native `AppRegistry.registerComponent`.

- `App.tsx`: This is the React Native default app. You can make changes here and see them directly in your simulator. This file will be replaced by our example application later on.

By getting to know all these files, you already learned a lot about React Native. You saw that it contains real native projects with real native dependencies, uses a lot of useful tools, and has a single entry point.

The next step for our example application is to set up a working folder structure.

Structuring the example application

First, I always recommend creating an `src` folder for all of your JavaScript/TypeScript code. It is always a good idea to have all the code that belongs together in one place.

For our example app, we create the following three subfolders in the `src` folder:

- `@types`: In this folder, you place your TypeScript type declarations.

- `components`: This folder contains all reusable components.

- `containers`: Here, you have containers that are used to define the **user interface (UI)** structure of your views. Typically, you put things such as `ScrollView` containers with custom animations here. These containers are used to hold the content of your views.

- `services`: In this folder, we'll create our services to connect to the movies. In this example, it will use the static JSON file as the source; later, we'll connect to an external **application programming interface (API)**.

- `views`: This folder contains whole-page views. In our case, it is the three views defined before.

> **Note**
>
> There are other approaches to how to structure a React Native project. Especially for large-scale projects, with multiple repositories, there can be ones that work better in some cases. You'll learn about some of them in *Chapter 10, Structuring Large-Scale, Multi-Platform Projects*. For our example project, this structure is absolutely fine.

To get a deeper understanding of what's going on, we try to do the first version of our example project completely without any third-party libraries. This is only for learning purposes and is not recommended in real-world projects.

The first thing we must decide on is the general architecture of the app. It can be very helpful to visualize the different parts of the application in a diagram, like the one you can see here:

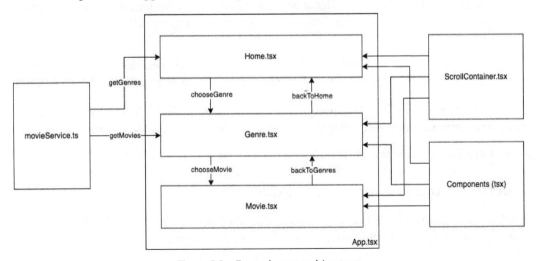

Figure 3.2 – Example app architecture

As you can see in *Figure 3.2*, we will create three views (`Home.tsx`, `Genre.tsx`, and `Movie.tsx`). Since we are not using any navigation library, we must use the state of `App.tsx` to switch between these views. All three views use the `ScrollContainer` container to correctly place the views' content. They also share some reusable components.

The result is a very simple app that lets us navigate our movie content. In the following screenshot, you can see what it looks like:

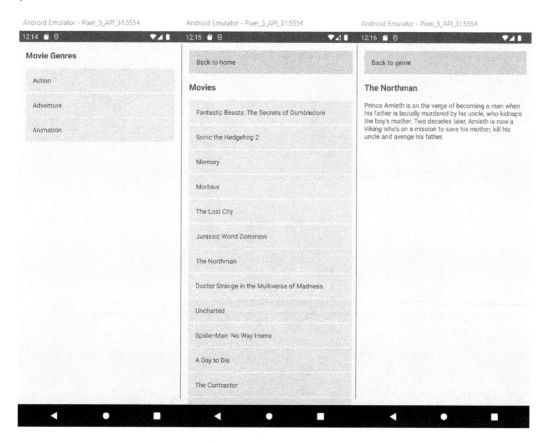

Figure 3.3 – Example app screenshot

You can see a list of movie genres on the first page, a list of movies of a single genre on the second page, and movie details on the third page.

Now you've learned about the architecture and seen a high-level overview, it's now time to dive deeper into the code. We'll focus on the most interesting parts, but if you want to see the whole code, please go to the GitHub repository mentioned in the *Technical requirements* section. Let's start with the `App.tsx` file.

Creating a root view

The App.tsx file serves as the root component of our project. It decides which view should be mounted and holds the global application state. Please have a look at the following code:

```tsx
const App = () => {
  const [page, setPage] = useState<number>(PAGES.HOME);
  const [genre, setGenre] = useState<IGenre |
      undefined>(undefined);
  const [movie, setMovie] = useState<IMovie |
      undefined>(undefined);
  const chooseGenre = (lGenre: IGenre) => {
    setGenre(lGenre);
    setPage(PAGES.GENRE);
  };
  const chooseMovie = (lMovie: IMovie) => {
    setMovie(lMovie);
    setPage(PAGES.MOVIE);
  };
  const backToGenres = () => {
    setMovie(undefined);
    setPage(PAGES.GENRE);
  };
  const backToHome = () => {
    setMovie(undefined);
    setGenre(undefined);
    setPage(PAGES.HOME);
  };
  switch (page) {
    case PAGES.HOME:
      return <Home chooseGenre={chooseGenre} />;
    case PAGES.GENRE:
      return (
        <Genre
          backToHome={backToHome}
          genre={genre}
          chooseMovie={chooseMovie}
```

```
            />
        );
    case PAGES.MOVIE:
        return <Movie backToGenres={backToGenres}
            movie={movie} />;
    }
};
```

As you can see here, the App.tsx file has three state variables. This state can be seen as a global state because the App.tsx file is the root component of the app and can be passed down to the other components. It must contain a page that defines which view should be visible, and it can hold a genre and a movie.

At the end of the file, you can find a switch/case statement. Based on the page state, this switch/case decides which view should be mounted. Also, the App.tsx file provides some functions to navigate through the application (chooseGenre, chooseMovie, backToGenres, backToHome) and passes them down to the views.

> **Important hint**
>
> As you can see, the direct setter functions of the state variables (setPage, setGenre, setMovie) aren't passed down to any view. Instead, we created functions that call these setter functions. This is best practice because it guarantees that our state is mutated in a predictable way. You should never allow your state to get mutated directly from outside your component. You will learn more about this in *Chapter 5, Managing States and Connecting Backends*.

Next, let's have a look at the views. These are pages that display content.

Displaying content based on a state

The Home view is the first page the user sees when opening the app. Please have a look at the following code:

```
import {getGenres} from '../../services/movieService';
interface HomeProps {
    chooseGenre: (genre: IGenre) => void;
}
const Home = (props: HomeProps) => {
    const [genres, setGenres] = useState<IGenre[]>([]);
    useEffect(() => {
        setGenres(getGenres());
```

```
  }, []);
  return (
    <ScrollContainer>
      <Header text="Movie Genres" />
      {genres.map(genre => {
        return (
          <Pressable onPress={() =>
                props.chooseGenre(genre)}>
            <Text style={styles.genreTitle}>{genre.name}
                </Text>
          </Pressable>
        );
      })}
    </ScrollContainer>
  );
};
```

Here, you can see multiple things. At the top of the code block, you can see that we defined an `interface` for the `props` component. This is the TypeScript declaration of what should be passed down to this component from the parent component (in this case, the `App.tsx` file). Next, we have a list of genres as state variables.

This is a local state or component state because it is only used inside this component. In the next line, we use the `useEffect` hook to call the `getGenres` method of our `movieService` to fetch the genres and set them to the local state.

You will learn more about the `useState` and `useEffect` hooks in the *Understanding class components, function components, and Hooks* section of this chapter, but for now, it is only important that `useEffect` with an empty array as the second argument is called once when the component gets mounted.

> **Note**
>
> When working with React, the terms *mounting* and *unmounting* are used a lot. **Mounting** means adding components to the render tree that weren't there before. A newly mounted component can trigger its lifecycle functions (class components) or hooks (function components). **Unmounting** means removing components from the render tree. This can also trigger lifecycle functions (class components) or Hook cleanups (function components).

After the `useEffect` Hook, you can see the `return` statement, which contains the **JavaScript XML (JSX)** that describes the UI. We use our `ScrollContainer` container, which contains the `Header` component and a list of `Pressable` instances, one for each genre. This list is created with the `.map` command.

> **Important note**
>
> This mixing of declarative UI and JavaScript data processing is one of the biggest strengths of React and React Native, and you will see it a lot. But whenever you do it, keep in mind that this is processed and recalculated every time the component is re-rendered. This means no expensive data processing operations should be done here.

After looking at the `Home` view, we should also have a look at the `Genre` view. It basically works the same way, but with one big difference. The `Genre` view fetches its data based on a property that is passed from the `App.tsx` file. Look at the `useEffect` hook of the `Genre.tsx` file here:

```
useEffect(() => {
    if (typeof props.genre !== 'undefined') {
        setMovies(getMoviesByGenreId(props.genre.id));
    }
}, [props.genre]);
```

You can see that the `getMoviesByGenreId` method of `movieService` needs a genre **identifier (ID)**. This is taken from the genre that is passed down to the `Genre.tsx` file from the `App.tsx` file.

The whole process works as follows:

1. The `App.tsx` file passes down a `chooseGenre` function to the `Home.tsx` file.
2. The user clicks on a genre and triggers the `chooseGenre` function, which sets the genre to the `App.tsx` state and also sets the page to GENRE in the `App.tsx` file, which unmounts `Home.tsx` and mounts `Genre.tsx`.
3. The `App.tsx` file passes down the genre to the `Genre.tsx` file.
4. The `Genre.tsx` file fetches the genre's movies based on the genre ID.

The same pattern is used to set the movie and navigate to the `Movie.tsx` view.

The `Movie.tsx` page does not fetch any data on its own in this example. It gets passed down the movie data it displays from the `App.tsx` file and needs no other information.

After understanding the views, we'll now have a look at the components.

Using reusable components

It is very important to move UI code that you use in different places to components, at least when the project grows—this is crucial to prevent duplicate code and an inconsistent UI. But even in a smaller project, using reusable components is always a good idea and speeds up development a lot. In this simple example, we created a `Header` component:

```
interface HeaderProps {
  text: string;
}
const Header = (props: HeaderProps) => {
  return <Text style={styles.title}>{props.text}</Text>;
};
const styles = StyleSheet.create({
  title: {
    fontSize: 18,
    fontWeight: 'bold',
    marginBottom: 16,
  },
});
```

As you can see, this is a very simple component. It takes a string and renders the string in a predefined way, but even this simple component saves us quite some time and prevents duplicated code. Instead of having to style the header text in `Home.tsx`, `Genre.tsx`, and `Movie.tsx`, we can just use the `Header` component and get our header text styled in a consistent way.

> **Important note**
>
> Use reusable components wherever you can. They ensure a consistent UI and make changes easily adaptable throughout the whole application.

After looking at the components, we'll turn our attention to the services next.

Using services to fetch data

You should always abstract the data fetching from the rest of the application. This is not only for logical reasons, but also if you have to change anything here (because of an API change), you don't want to touch your views or components.

In this example, we use two JSON files as the data source. You can find them in the repository under `assets/data`. The services use the files to filter or list the data and provide it to the views. Please have a look at the following code:

```
const genres: IGenre[] = require('../../assets/data/genres.
json');
const movies: IMovie[] = require('../../assets/data/movies.
json');
const getGenres = (): Array<IGenre> => {
  return genres;
};
const getMovies = (): Array<IMovie> => {
  return movies;
};
const getMovieByGenreId = (genreId: number):
    Array<IMovie> => {
        return movies.filter(movie =>
            movie.genre_ids.indexOf(genreId) > -1);
};
export {getGenres, getMovies, getMovieByGenreId };
```

As you can see here, we require the two JSON files in the first two lines. The `getGenres` and `getMovies` functions just return the content of the files, without any filtering. `getMovieByGenreId` takes a numeric genre ID and filters the movies for this ID in the `genre_ids` of the movie. It then returns the filtered `movies` array.

In the last line, we export the functions to be importable in our views.

> **Important note**
>
> In larger projects, it is very common to start working with dummy data such as our JSON files here. This is because the frontend part is often developed in parallel to the API, and with the dummy data, the frontend team exactly knows what the data will look like. When the API is ready and the data service is well abstracted, it is no problem to replace the dummy data with the real-world API data fetching. We'll also do this in *Chapter 5, Managing States and Connecting Backends*.

At last, we'll have a look at the containers.

Using containers for page styling

In our example, we only have one container, `ScrollContainer`. It has a very similar purpose to the components, but while components are mainly parts that are used as parts of a view, containers are used to define the (outer) layout of a view. Please have a look at the code of our `ScrollContainer` container here:

```
interface ScrollContainerProps {
  children: React.ReactNode;
}
const ScrollContainer = (props: ScrollContainerProps) => {
  return (
    <SafeAreaView style={styles.backgroundStyle}>
      <ScrollView
        contentInsetAdjustmentBehavior="automatic"
        contentContainerStyle={styles.contentContainer}
        style={styles.backgroundStyle}>
        {props.children}
      </ScrollView>
    </SafeAreaView>
  );
};
```

As you can see in the interface definition, our `ScrollContainer` container takes only one property called `children`, which is defined as `React.ReactNode`. This means you can pass components to `ScrollContainer`. Also, the `children` property of a React component makes it possible to use this component with opening and closing tags while passing all JSX between the tags down to the component as a `children` property. This is exactly what we have done in all our views.

Our `ScrollContainer` container also uses a component called `SafeAreaView`. This is provided by React Native and handles all the different devices with notches (iPhone, Samsung), virtual back buttons (Android), and more.

Now that you've had a look at all the different parts of our first example application, it's time for a short wrap-up. Up to now, you've learned how to structure an application, why it is important to abstract the different layers, and how to create reusable UI.

You've also learned that React and React Native components always consist of two parts: preparing the data in state/props and displaying the data with JSX. Maybe you also have realized that all our components are sorted in such a way that the data preparation is at the top of the component while the displaying of the data is at the bottom. I prefer this way of structuring a component because it makes it much more readable.

You also already know a way to pass properties between components. Because this is a very important topic, we'll focus on that in more detail in the next section.

Passing properties

As you have already seen in the example application, there are multiple ways to pass data around in an application. Some best practices have been established that you should definitely stick to; otherwise, your application can get very hard to debug and maintain. We list these here:

- **Never modify a component state in an unpredictable way from outside the component**: I know—I repeat myself; we had this in the previous section, but this is very important. Modifying your state in an unpredictable way from outside the component can lead to bad errors, especially when you are working on a large project with a team of developers. But let's have a look in detail.

  Unpredictable in this scenario means that you pass the setter function of your state directly to other components.

  Why is this so bad? Because other components and maybe other developers can decide what to put in the state of your component. It is very likely that sooner or later, one of them decides to put something in there that your component can't handle in some edge cases.

  What is the solution? There are multiple scenarios where you have to modify a component state from outside the component, but if you have to, do it in a predictable way by passing predefined functions. These functions should then verify the data and handle the state modification.

- **Always use type declarations for your props**: You should always use any kind of type declaration for your component props so that other developers know what kind of data your component expects. I recommend using TypeScript, but if you use plain JavaScript, there is a library called `PropTypes` you can use. For more information, please look at this link: `https://www.npmjs.com/package/prop-types`.

- **Limit the number of props you pass**: The more properties you pass, the harder your code will get to read and maintain, so think twice if it is necessary to pass a property. Also, it's better to pass objects rather than multiple primitives.

After these best practices for passing properties, we'll have a deeper look at different component types and hooks in the next section.

Understanding class components, function components, and Hooks

React and React Native provide two different ways to write components: class components and function components. Nowadays, you can use both variants interchangeably. Both ways are supported, and there is no sign that one of them won't be supported in the future. So, why do two different ways exist? This is due to historical reasons. Before hooks were introduced in 2019 (React 16.8), function components couldn't have a state or use any lifecycle methods, which meant that any component that needed to fetch and store data had to be a class component. But because function components require less code to write, they were often used for displaying data that was passed as props.

The limitation of function components changed with the introduction of Hooks. **Hooks** are functions provided by React that make it possible to use functionality, which was limited to class components, also in function components.

Today, it depends a lot on your preferences as to whether you work with function components and hooks or class components and lifecycle methods. Again, function components are less code to write, but developers with experience in **object-oriented programming** (**OOP**) languages might prefer to work with class components. Both ways are totally fine and don't differ in terms of performance. Only the app size will be a little larger when working with class components.

In the next subsections, we'll have a look at the different syntax and how to work with the different component types. We'll start with class components.

Working with class components and lifecycle methods

As already mentioned, class components were always able to hold dynamic data in a changeable state. This state can be changed due to either user interaction or an action triggered in a lifecycle method. Lifecycle methods are methods that are provided by React and are called at a specific time of the component execution.

One of the most important lifecycle methods is componentDidMount. This method is called directly after a component was mounted and is often used for data fetching. The following code example shows a very basic example of a class component:

```
class App extends React.Component {
  constructor() {
    super();
    this.state = {
        num: Math.random() * 100
    };
  }
  render() {
    return <Text>This is a random number:
        {this.state.num}</Text>;
  }
}
```

The class component has one state property that is initialized in the constructor of the class. This state variable can hold multiple objects. In this case, it only contains a num property that gets initialized with a random number between 0 and 100. The component always has to have a render function. This function contains the JSX of the component. In this example, it's only a Text component that displays a random number to the user.

To bring some life to this example, we can start an interval to regenerate the random number every second. This is where lifecycle functions come into play. We would use the componentDidMount lifecycle function to start the interval and componentWillUnmount to clean it up. Please have a look at the following code snippet:

```
componentDidMount = () => {
  this.interval = setInterval(() => {
    this.setState({ num: Math.random() * 100 });
  }, 1000);
};
componentWillUnmount = () => {
  clearInterval(this.interval);
};
```

In componentDidMount, we create an interval that updates the num state every second. As you can see, we are not setting the state directly, but we are using the setState method. Remember— setting the state directly is only allowed for initialization in the constructor.

We also store the interval's handle to this.interval. In componentWillUnmount, we clear this.interval so that we don't have code running infinitely when we are navigating away from the component.

> **Note**
>
> componentDidMount is the right place to fetch data that is used in the component.

If you want to see a running version of this example, please have a look at the following CodeSandbox instance: https://codesandbox.io/s/class-component-basic-nz9cy?file=/src/index.js.

After this simple example, it's time to look at lifecycle methods a little closer. You'll now get to know the most used ones, as listed here:

- componentDidMount(): This method is called directly after a component is mounted. It is called only once during the whole lifecycle of a component. It can be used for data fetching, adding handlers, or populating the state in any other way.

- `componentWillUnmount()`: This method is called directly before a component gets unmounted. It is called only once during the whole lifecycle of a component. It should be used for cleaning up handlers, intervals, timeouts, or any other executing code.

- `componentDidUpdate(prevProps)`: This method is called every time a component gets updated and re-rendered. It can be called multiple times (a lot of times) during the whole lifecycle of a component. `componentDidUpdate` gets the previous props passed as a parameter so that you can compare them to the current props to check what changed. It can be used for refetching data based on changed parameters of the component. Please be informed that any `setState` method in the `componentDidUpdate` method has to be wrapped in a condition. This is for preventing infinite loops.

- `shouldComponentUpdate(nextProps, nextState)`: This method is called every time before a re-render will take place. It can be called multiple times (a lot of times) during the whole lifecycle of a component. It exists only for performance reasons, because in some scenarios, you only want to re-render a component when specific parts of props or state are changing. This can be especially useful when working with large applications or large lists of data.

There are some more lifecycle methods that aren't used that often. If you want to check them out, please have a look at the official documentation here: `https://reactjs.org/docs/react-component.html`.

In this subsection, you learned the syntax of class components and how to work with lifecycle methods. To have a direct comparison, we'll write the same example for function components with Hooks in the next subsection.

Working with function components and Hooks

You should already be familiar with the function component syntax since we were using it for the example app in the first section of this chapter. Nevertheless, we'll have a look at a code example, as we did in the previous subsection about class components, as follows:

```
const App = () => {
  const [num, setNum] = useState(Math.random() * 100);
  return <Text>This is a random number: {num}</Text>;
};
```

As you can see, even in this small example, the code is much shorter. A function component is basically nothing else than a function that runs on every re-render. But with Hooks, especially the `useState` hook, function components provide a way of storing data between re-renders.

We use the `useState` hook to store our num variable in the component state. Function components have to return what should be rendered. You can think of the component as a direct `render` function. We can then use the num variable to print the random number.

> **Important hint**
>
> All code that you put in a function component without using Hooks or similar mechanisms runs on every re-render. It is basically the same as putting code in the `render` function of a class component. This means you should only put your declarative UI and cheap data processing operations there. All other operations should be wrapped with Hooks, to prevent performance issues.

Next, we'll start an interval to change the random number every second. We did the same in the example with the class component. The following code does exactly this in a function component:

```
useEffect(() => {
  const interval = setInterval(() => {
    setNum(Math.random() * 100);
  }, 1000);
  return () => clearInterval(interval);
}, []);
```

We use the `useEffect` Hook to start the interval. The `useEffect` interval takes two arguments. The first one is a function that defines the effect that should be run. The second argument is an array, and it defines when the effect should be run. It is optional, and if you don't provide it, your effect will run on every re-render.

You can put state variables, other functions, and much more in there. If you do so, the effect will run every time one of the variables in this array changes. In our case, we want the effect to only run once when the component is mounted. To achieve this, we'll use an empty array as a second argument.

We also return an anonymous function that clears the interval in the effect. This is a cleanup function. This cleanup function runs when the component unmounts and before running the effect the next time. Since we only run the effect on mount, the cleanup function only runs on unmount.

If you want to run this example, please have a look at the following CodeSandbox instance: `https://codesandbox.io/s/function-component-basic-yhsrlo`.

After this simple example, it's time to take a deeper look at the most important Hooks. We already used two of them, which are by far the most important ones.

Working with stateless function components with useState

The `useState` Hook makes it possible to store information between re-renders. and create stateful function components. It returns an array with two entries. The first one is the state variable, while the second one is the setter function for the state variable. In most cases, you will use array destructuring to access both entries in one line, as in the following code example:

```
const [example, setExample] = useState(exampleDefaultValue)
```

The useState function also takes one argument that you can use to define the default value of the state variable. This is the value it gets initialized with.

To change the value of the state, you always have to use the setter function. Never set the value directly since this won't trigger any re-renders or other React internals.

To change the value and trigger a re-render, you can simply call the setter function with a fixed value. This is how it looks:

```
setExample(newValue)
```

This is what you'll do most of the time, but you also can pass an update function. This can be very useful when you have to do state updates based on the old state, like this:

```
setExample(prevValue => prevValue + 1)
```

In this example, we'll pass a function that takes the previous value as a single argument. We can now use this value to return the new value, which will then be used in the setter. This is especially useful when incrementing or decrementing values.

Now that we are able to store data between re-renders, we'll want to run some functions after certain events.

Using effects with useEffect

The useEffect Hook is used to run code after certain events. These events can be the mounting of a component or an update of a component. The first argument of the useEffect Hook has to be a function that will be run when the effect is triggered.

The second argument is an array that can be used to limit the events the effect should trigger on. It is optional, and when you don't provide it, the effect runs on mount and on every update that triggers a re-render. If you provide it as an empty array, the effect runs only on mount. If you provide values in the array, the effect is limited to running only if one of the provided values changes.

There is one very important thing to mention here. If you use references to variables and functions that can change between re-renders inside your useEffect Hook, you have to include them in the dependencies. This is because otherwise, you could have a reference to stale data in your useEffect Hook. Please have a look at the following diagram for an illustration of this:

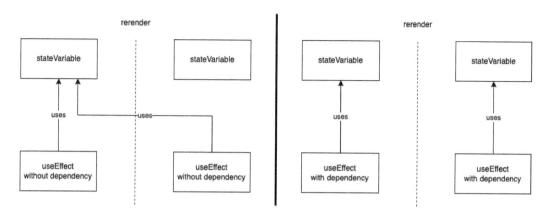

Figure 3.4 – References in useEffect

On the left side, you see what happens when you don't include a state variable—which you access inside your useEffect Hook—in the dependencies. In this case, the state variable changes and triggers a re-render, but since your useEffect Hook has no connection to the state variable, it does not know that there was a change.

When the effect runs the next time—for example, triggered by a change in another dependency—you'll access the stale (old) version of your state variable. This is very important to know because it can lead to very serious and hard-to-find bugs.

On the right side of the diagram, you see what happens when you include the state variable in the dependencies of the useEffect Hook. The useEffect Hook now knows when the state variable changes and updates the reference.

This is the same for functions that you write in your component. Please always keep in mind that every function that you write inside your function component that is not wrapped by a Hook will be recreated on every re-render.

That means if you want to access functions inside an useEffect Hook, you also have to add them to the dependencies. Otherwise, you'll potentially reference stale versions of these functions. But this leads to another problem. Since the functions are recreated on every re-render, it would trigger your effect on every re-render, and this is something we don't want most of the time.

This is where two other Hooks come into play. It is possible to memoize values and functions between re-renders, which not only solves our useEffect triggering problem but also improves performance significantly.

Improving performance with useCallback and useMemo

Both useCallback and useMemo are Hooks to memoize things between re-renders. While useCallback is provided to memoize a function, useMemo is provided to memoize a value.

The API of both Hooks is very similar. You provide a function and an array of dependencies. The `useCallback` Hook memoizes the function without executing it, while the `useMemo` Hook executes the function and memoizes the return value of the function.

Always keep in mind that these hooks are for performance optimization. Especially regarding `useMemo`, the React documentation explicitly state that there is no semantic guarantee that memoization works in every case. This means you have to write your code in a way that works even without memoization.

You now know the most common Hooks. You'll get to know some more in *Chapter 5*, *Managing States and Connecting Backends*. If you want to get a deeper understanding, I can recommend the official Hooks tutorial in the React documentation: `https://reactjs.org/docs/hooks-reference.html`.

> **Note**
>
> Besides the Hooks that are provided by React, you can write your own Hooks to share logic between function components. You can call all React Hooks inside your custom Hook. Please stick to the naming convention and always start your custom Hooks with `use`.

After this extensive look at components, Hooks, and how the React part of React Native works, it's now time to have a deeper look at the native part. As you learned in *Chapter 1*, *What Is React Native?*, React Native has a JavaScript part and a native part.

As you learned in the first section of this chapter, React Native ships with a complete Android project and a complete iOS project. It's time to have a look at how everything is tied together.

Connecting different platforms to JavaScript

In the first subsection of this section, we'll focus on Android and iOS because these are the most common platforms. At the end of this section, we'll also have a look at how to deploy to the web, Mac, Windows, and even other platforms.

First, it is important to understand that React Native provides a way of communication between JavaScript and Native. Most of the time, you don't need to change anything on the native side because the framework itself or some community libraries cover most of the native functionalities, but nevertheless, it is important to understand how it works.

Let's start with the UI. When you write your UI in JavaScript, React Native maps your JSX components such as `View` and `Text` to native components such as `UIView` and `NSAttributedString` on iOS or `android.view` and `SpannableString` on Android. The styling of these native components is done using a layout engine called Yoga.

While React Native provides a lot of components for Android and iOS, there are some scenarios that don't work out of the box. A good example of this is **Scalable Vector Graphics (SVG)**. React Native itself does not provide SVG support but React Native provides the logic it uses to connect JavaScript and native components so that everyone can create their own mappings and components.

And here comes the large React Native community into play. Nearly every feature is covered by an open source library that provides these mappings, at least for Android and iOS. That's also the case for SVG support. There is a well-maintained library called `react-native-svg`, which you can find here: `https://github.com/react-native-svg/react-native-svg`.

This library provides a `<SVG />` JavaScript component that under the hood maps to the native SVG implementations on Android and iOS.

After understanding how UI mapping works, it's time to have a look at other communication between JavaScript and Native. The second very common use case is the transfer of data such as information about user gestures, sensor information, or other data that can be created on one side and has to be transferred to the other side.

This is done through connected methods. React Native provides a way to call native methods from JavaScript, pass callback functions to Native, and call these callbacks from Native. This is how data can be transferred in both directions.

While Android and iOS support comes out of the box, React Native is not limited to these platforms. Microsoft created open source projects called `react-native-windows` and `react-native-macos`. There are a lot of features supported by these projects to bring your app to Windows and macOS.

There is also a very useful project called `react-native-web` that adds web support to React Native. One important thing to understand is that even if you could use the same code base for all platforms, you might want to adapt it to best practices for the particular platform.

For example, if you are targeting the web, you might want to optimize your project for search engines, something that is not necessary for Android and iOS apps. There are multiple approaches to handling these platform-specific adjustments. The most common ones will be explained in *Chapter 10, Structuring Large-Scale, Multi-Platform Projects*.

While you can use Android, iOS, Windows, macOS, and the web quite easily, you are not limited to them. Basically, you could use React Native to create apps for any platform, and you would only have to write the native part on your own.

For a long time, all communication between JavaScript and Native was done asynchronously via JSON over the so-called bridge. While this works fine for most cases, it can lead to performance issues in some cases.

Therefore, the React Native core team at Facebook decided to completely rewrite the React Native Architecture. It took a couple of years, but at the time of writing this book, the new architecture is rolled out at the main Facebook app, and it also landed in the React Native open source repository to be publicly available. You will learn more about the new architecture in the next section.

Introducing the new React Native Architecture

In the last section, you learned how the connection between JavaScript and Native works in general. While this general idea does not change, the underlying implementation changes completely. Please have a look at the following diagram:

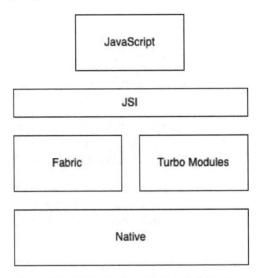

Figure 3.5 – The new React Native Architecture

The core of the new React Native Architecture is something called **JavaScript Interface (JSI)**. It replaces the old way of communication via the bridge. While communication over the bridge was done with serialized JSON in an asynchronous way, JSI makes it possible for *JavaScript to hold references to C++ host objects and invoke methods on them.*

This means the JavaScript object and the C++ host object connected via JSI will be really aware of each other, which makes synchronous communication possible and makes the need for JSON serialization obsolete. This results in a huge performance boost for all React Native apps.

Another part of the rearchitecture is a new renderer called Fabric, which reduces the number of steps done to create a native UI. Also, using JSI, a shadow tree that determines what will be rendered is created directly in C++, while JavaScript also has a reference to it. This means JavaScript and Native can both interact with the shadow tree, which massively improves the responsiveness of the UI.

The second part of the rearchitecture that benefits from JSI is called **Turbo Modules**. It replaces Native Modules, which was the way to connect native modules and JavaScript modules. While the old Native Modules all had to be initialized at startup because JavaScript had no information about the state of the native module, JSI makes it possible to delay the initialization of the module until it is needed.

Since JavaScript can now hold a direct reference, there is also no need to work with serialized JSON. This results in a significant boost in the startup time for React Native apps.

There is also a new developer tool called **CodeGen** that gets introduced with the new architecture. It uses typed JavaScript to generate corresponding native interface files, to ensure compatibility between JavaScript and the native side. This is very useful when writing own libraries with native code. You will learn more about this in *Chapter 10, Structuring Large-Scale, Multi-Platform Projects*, in the Creating Own Libraries section.

All in all, the new architecture will bring a huge performance boost on all levels for every React Native app. It will take some time to switch an existing app to the new architecture, and it also will take some time until all common open source libraries have done the switch. But it will happen sooner or later, and it will definitely be worth the work.

Summary

To end this chapter, let's have a short summary of what this chapter was about. You learned about what the project structure of a simple React Native app looks like and what the different files are for. You also know about class components and function components, and you understand the most important lifecycle methods and Hooks. Based on this, you can use component states and trigger code execution in both class components and function components.

You also learned how JavaScript and Native are connected in React Native apps, what the problems are with the current (old) React Native Architecture, and what the new architecture is.

Now that you have a good overview of how React Native works in general, let's dive deeper into components, styling, storage, and navigation in the next chapter.

Part 2:
Building World-Class Apps
with React Native

In this part, we will focus on not only creating apps but creating first-class apps with React Native. You will learn what you must pay attention to when working with React Native to create apps with native performance and a world-class user experience.

The following chapters are in this section:

- *Chapter 4, Styling, Storage, and Navigation in React Native*

- *Chapter 5, Managing States and Connecting Backends*

- *Chapter 6, Working with Animations*

- *Chapter 7, Handling Gestures in React Native*

- *Chapter 8, JavaScript Engines and Hermes*

- *Chapter 9, Essential Tools for Improving React Native Development*

4
Styling, Storage, and Navigation in React Native

Now that you know the general concepts behind React Native, it's time to have a deeper look at the most common areas of React Native.

This chapter covers different areas, all of which are important when working with React Native. When creating a large app with React Native, you always have to have a good understanding of how the styling of your app works to create a beautiful product. Besides styling, there is another thing that decides if users will like your app from an aesthetic point of view – **animation**. However, this will be covered in *Chapter 6, Working with Animations*.

Another thing we will focus on in this chapter is how to store data locally on users' devices. Every platform works differently. While Android and iOS are quite similar and you can get access to the device's storage with huge capacity, this is completely different when working with the web, where capacity is very limited.

The last thing we'll cover is how to navigate between screens in your React Native app. Again, this can differ from platform to platform, but you'll get a good overview of the different navigation concepts.

In this chapter, we will cover the following topics:

- Understanding how to style a React Native app
- Using local storage solutions in React Native
- Understanding navigation in React Native

Technical requirements

To be able to run the code in this chapter, you must set up the following:

- A working React Native environment (`https://reactnative.dev/docs/environment-setup` – React Native CLI Quickstart)
- While most of this chapter should also work on Windows, I recommend working on a Mac

Understanding how to style a React Native app

You can choose from different solutions to handle styling in your React Native app. But before we take a look at the most common ones, you must understand the underlying concepts. The first thing we'll cover in this chapter is what all these solutions try to achieve.

Make styling maintainable

Styling is often handled very poorly when a project starts because it does not interfere with the business logic, so it isn't likely to introduce bugs. So, most of the time, when thinking about the architecture of an application, most developers think of state management, data flow, component structure, and more, but not about styling. This always takes its toll when a project grows. It starts to take more and more time to keep a consistent design and making changes to your UI becomes a real pain.

Therefore, you should think about how to handle styling in your application right at the beginning. No matter what solution or library you use, you should always stick to the following concepts:

- **Use a central file for colors, fonts, and sizes**: This should either be a single file or one file for colors, one for fonts, and one for sizes such as margins, paddings, and border radiuses. I prefer to use a single file.
- **Never hardcode values in your components/CSS files**: You should never use fixed values inside your component. Always use the values you define in your central file. This guarantees that your UI stays consistent and that you can easily change the values if you have to adapt.
- **Never duplicate code**: When you catch yourself copying the styling of parts of a component because it's easier, faster, or more convenient, always keep in mind that it isn't in the long run. Duplicate code always leads to inconsistencies in the UI and makes you have to touch multiple files when you want to change something later. So, instead of copying and pasting your code, extract it to a component or styles file. You will learn more about these options later.

When we come back to our example project with these concepts, we will have to refactor it because, at the moment, we violate all of these concepts. We have no central file; we have hardcoded values everywhere and we have a `backButton` style defined in multiple files.

First, let's create a central file to store our values. This could look like this:

```
import {Appearance} from 'react-native';
const isDarkMode = Appearance.getColorScheme() === 'dark';
const FontConstants = {
  familyRegular: 'sans-serif',
  sizeTitle: 18,
  sizeRegular: 14,
  weightBold: 'bold',
};
const ColorConstants = {
  background: isDarkMode ? '#333333' : '#efefef',
  backgroundMedium: isDarkMode ? '#666666' : '#dddddd',
  font: isDarkMode ? '#eeeeee' : '#222222',
};
const SizeConstants = {
  paddingSmall: 2,
  paddingRegular: 8,
  paddingLarge: 16,
  borderRadius: 8,
};
export {FontConstants, ColorConstants, SizeConstants};
```

As you can see, we have all our values in one single place. If you take a deeper look, we also introduced dark mode to our app, which was a 3-minute task with our central color store. We only have to get the information about the device appearance settings and deliver the colors accordingly.

> **Note**
>
> You can test your app in dark mode very easily on the iOS Simulator. Go to **Settings**, scroll to the bottom, and choose **Developer**. The **Developer** screen will open; the first toggle activates **Dark Appearance**. If you support dark mode with our app, you should always test on two simulators – one in the dark mode and one in the light mode.

Now that we have our central store, let's create a `<BackButton />` component to get rid of the duplicated style definitions. This can look like this:

```
interface BackButtonProps{
  text: string;
  onPress: () => void;
}
const BackButton = (props: BackButtonProps) => {
  return (
    <Pressable onPress={props.onPress}
      style={styles.backButton}>
      <Text>{props.text}</Text>
    </Pressable>
  );
};
const styles = StyleSheet.create({
  backButton: {
    padding: SizeConstants.paddingLarge,
    marginBottom: SizeConstants.paddingLarge,
    backgroundColor: ColorConstants.backgroundMedium,
  },
});
```

In our newly created component, we don't use fixed values anymore, but we are referencing the values in our central store.

Lastly, we have to go through our app, replace the `backButton` pressables with our new component, and replace the fixed values with references to our central store. With that, we have complied with the concepts.

These concepts are the core of different libraries or solutions. To choose the right solution for your project, one of the most important decisions is which platform to deploy to. The following subsection will cover the most common solutions, including information about which platform the solution works best on.

Choosing the right styling solution

In this subsection, we'll have a look at inline styling, React Native StyleSheets, CSS modules, and styled-components. All four solutions work well and have their benefits and drawbacks. We'll start with inline styles.

Using React Native inline styles

To understand inline styles, let's have a look at a code example. The following code shows the `<Header / >` component from our example project from the previous chapter but it uses inline styles to style the `Text` component:

```
const Header = (props: HeaderProps) => {
    return <Text style={{
            fontSize: 18,
            fontWeight: 'bold',
            marginBottom: 16}
        }>
            {props.text}
        </Text>;
};
```

As you can see, we can just create an object with the styling rules. This works and has a big advantage. Not only can you use fixed values, but you can also use any static or dynamic value you can access in your component. This can be very useful, especially when you are working with user-defined themes. But this approach also comes with multiple disadvantages.

First, the code gets quite confusing when the project grows – at least, I think the code is hard to read when styling, components, and data are mixed in that way. So, I would always prefer to separate this as much as possible.

Next, you cannot reuse any styling. You must copy your styles every time you need them again. Now, you could argue that you wouldn't have to copy the styles because you can simply extract the component that includes the style into a custom component. Although this is correct, there are some cases where you don't want to do this. We'll have a deeper look at these scenarios in the next subsection.

Next, we must think about performance. Inline style objects will be recreated at every render, which can negatively impact the performance and memory usage of your app.

Last, we'll have a look at the different platforms. This inline style approach has very little room for optimization on build time for the different platforms. While this may be no real problem on Android, iOS, Windows, and macOS, it can become a real pain for the web because it makes your bundle size a lot larger.

On the web, you must think about load times a lot because the user has no installed version of your application. Also, search engines such as Google care a lot about load times, and it will affect your ranking positively or negatively. So, your styling code must be optimized during the build process, which is not possible with inline styles.

To take advantage of optimization, you'll have to use StyleSheets. We'll have a look at them next.

Using React Native StyleSheets

We used StyleSheets in our example app in the previous chapter, but we'll have a look at them again here to truly understand their benefits. Not only do they make the code more readable and support a good separation of styling and business logic, but they also make it possible to use a lot of performance optimization at the build time and runtime of your app.

The following code is for the `<Header />` component from our example app. It uses React Native StyleSheets for styling:

```
const Header = (props: HeaderProps) => {
  return <Text style={styles.title}>{props.text}</Text>;
};
const styles = StyleSheet.create({
  title: {
    fontSize: 18,
    fontWeight: 'bold',
    marginBottom: 16,
  },
});
```

There are multiple things you should realize when looking at this code:

- First, it is much clearer and better separated.
- Second, `StyleSheet` is defined outside of the component, which makes it persist between rerenders. This is better in terms of performance and memory usage.
- Third, `StyleSheet.create` will create errors in your simulator when you are using styles that can't be interpreted. This can be very useful for catching bugs at a very early stage.

But the biggest benefit of StyleSheets is the possibility to optimize your styling code for the web. The open source web library known as react-native-web does a great job of splitting all the StyleSheets of your application into classes and adding the needed class names to your components. This makes your code small and optimized and improves your load time a lot.

Besides all these benefits, there is one problem with StyleSheets. Since they are declared outside of your component, you cannot access your component variables, such as state and props. This means that if you want to use a user-generated value in your styling, you have to combine your StyleSheet values with inline styles, like this:

```
<Text style={[styles.title, {color:props.color}]}>{props.
text}</Text>
```

This code would use the `title` style from the StyleSheet and add a user-defined color to the `<Text />` component. This combined approach can also be used when working with animations. You can read more about this in *Chapter 6, Working with Animations*.

Last, we'll have a look at another benefit of StyleSheets. You can use a style multiple times in your component. Again, if you stick to my recommendations, you will never have to do that because you will be creating a custom component in these scenarios. But for daily work, there are circumstances where it is faster to not create a component and where it also does not hurt.

For example, if you have a simple component with two lines of text, you can either create a `<TextLine />` component and use it two times, or simply use two `<Text />` components with the same style reference in a StyleSheet.

This first approach with the `<TextLine />` component is the cleaner one, but the second approach will save you some time and does not create problems in the long run. So, in this case, StyleSheets have another benefit versus inline styles.

> **Note**
>
> Always be careful when you use the same style multiple times. While it can be useful, in many cases, you duplicate code that should be extracted into a custom component.

Now that we understand this built-in solution, let's look at two solutions that need external libraries.

Styling with CSS modules

CSS modules are very popular on the web. You use CSS, Sass, or Less to style your components. In most cases, you would end up having one additional style file per component. Experts often argue if that's good or bad.

You have an additional file, but you have a clear separation between styling and components. I do like the separation, but if you manage to split your application into small components, adding the style directly to the component is fine from my point of view.

Using CSS modules in React Native needs some additional configuration. Since React Native does not have a built-in CSS processor, you must transform your CSS code into JavaScript styles before it can be displayed. This can be done with the babel transformer.

CSS modules can be a great choice if you share your styles between React (the web) and React Native projects, without using react-native-web to generate the web part. This is especially true when you are building an app for an existing web application.

One very important problem with this approach is that you can't use your JavaScript variables in your CSS modules. Even though you can create and use CSS variables, this does not enable you to use user-generated values in your styles.

If you start a green field project for Android, iOS, Windows, or Mac, I wouldn't recommend using CSS modules since, for these platforms, the CSS module approach has no benefits over StyleSheets. Again, the only scenario where I would recommend using CSS modules is when you build an app for an existing web application that is based on CSS modules.

There is also another solution that is very popular for React web projects that can be used in React Native. It's called **styled-components** and you'll learn about it in the next subsection.

Understanding styled-components

styled-components is a very popular library for styling React web applications. It also has very good support for React Native and can be a good choice in some cases. The styled-component approach uses the component approach through to the end. Instead of styling the primitive components such as View and Text, you enhance them with tagged template literals to create new components, called styled-components.

The following code shows the <Header /> component in our example project but styled with styled-components:

```
import styled from 'styled-components/native';
const Header = (props: HeaderProps) => {
  return <StyledText>{props.text}</StyledText>;
};
const StyledText = styled.Text`
  font-size: ${FontConstants.sizeTitle};
  font-weight: ${FontConstants.weightBold};
  margin-bottom: ${SizeConstants.paddingLarge};
  color: ${ColorConstants.font};
`;
```

As you can see, we create the StyledText component by using styled from styled-components and add a template literal to the React Native Text component. Inside this literal, we can write plain CSS. The cool thing here is that we can also use JavaScript variables and we can even pass props to our styled-component. This would look like this:

```
<StyledText primary>{props.text}</StyledText>;
```

This is how we would pass a property to our StyledText component. Now, we can use this property inside our template literal:

```
const StyledText = styled.Text`
  font-size: ${props => props.primary ?
```

```
          FontConstants.sizeTitle :
          FontConstants.sizeRegular};
    `;
```

This function is called **interpolation** and makes it possible to use user-generated content inside the CSS of our styled-components.

This is awesome because it solves a lot of problems, supports a clear separation between structure and styling, and allows us to use regular CSS, which is more familiar to most developers than the camel-cased CSS in the JavaScript of StyleSheets.

While I like this approach for the web, I remain critical of it for app-only projects. The styled-components library has a lot of useful optimization features for the web, but on pure React Native projects, it also compiles to CSS in JavaScript styles. In addition, it doesn't provide support for animations, which is a very important part of modern apps. You can read more about this in *Chapter 6, Working with Animations*.

Although I wouldn't recommend using styled-components for pure React Native projects, they can be very useful when you try to share your styling code between React Native and React projects, without using react-native-web. In this case, you can benefit from styled-components a lot.

If you want to have a deeper look at styled-components, I recommend reading the official documentation at `https://styled-components.com/docs`.

In this section, we learned the most important concepts of styling your React Native app and looked at the most common solutions to implement the styles. Most of the time, you wouldn't write all your styles on your own but use a UI library. This will be handled in *Chapter 9, Essential Tools for Improving React Native Development*.

If you want to see all changes to the example project, please have a look at the repository for this example project and choose the `chapter-4-styling` tag.

Now that we know how to style our app, it's time to store some data on the user's device.

Using local storage solutions in React Native

Storing data locally is a very important task in mobile apps. Even nowadays, you cannot be sure that a mobile device is always connected to the internet. Because of this, it is best practice to create your app in such a way that it has as much functionality as possible, even without a connection to the internet. That said, you can see why storing data locally is important for React Native apps.

The most important criterion for differentiation for local storage solutions is if it is a secure or an unsecure storage solution. Since most apps store at least some information about the user, you should always think about which information you want to put in which store.

> **Important**
> Always use a secure storage solution to store sensitive information.

While it is important to store sensitive data in a secure store, most data, such as user progress, app content, and more, can be stored in a *normal* storage solution. Secure storage operations always come with some overhead due to encryption/decryption and/or accessing special device functionalities, so you should only use them for sensitive information to prevent a negative impact on your app's performance.

In the following subsection, you will learn about the most common storage solutions for normal data.

Storing non-sensitive data

For a long time, React Native shipped with its built-in storage solution called AsyncStorage. But since the React Native core team at Facebook tried to reduce the React Native core to the minimum (lean core), AsyncStorage was handed over to the community for further development.

Nevertheless, it is very well maintained and most likely the most used storage solution. Besides AsyncStorage, other common solutions include `react-native-mmkv/react-native-mmkv-storage`, `react-native-sqlite-storage/react-native-quick-sqlite` and `react-native-fs`. All these solutions have their strengths and weaknesses, work completely differently, and can be used for slightly different tasks. Let's start with the most popular one.

Working with AsyncStorage

AsyncStorage is a simple key/value store that can be used to store data. While it can only store primitive data, you must serialize complex objects to JSON before storing them. Nevertheless, it is very simple to use. The API looks like this:

```
import AsyncStorage from '@react-native-async-storage/async-
storage';
// set item
const jsonValue = JSON.stringify(value)
await AsyncStorage.setItem('@key', jsonValue)
// get item
const strValue = await AsyncStorage.getItem('@key')
const jsonValue = strValue != null ? JSON.parse(strValue) :
null
```

As you can see, there are very simple APIs for setting and getting data.

`AsyncStorage` is not encrypted and cannot be used to run complex queries. It is a simple key/value store; there is no database. Also, it does not support transactions or locking. This means you have to be extremely careful when you write/read to/from different parts of your application.

I recommend using it to store user progress, information about app content, and any other data that does not have to be searchable. For more information on installing and using `AsyncStorage`, please look at the official documentation at `https://react-native-async-storage.github.io/async-storage/docs/install/`.

A relatively new alternative to `AsyncStorage` is MMKV for React Native. It is up to 30 times faster and comes with a lot more features.

Working with MMKV in React Native

MMKV is a native storage solution developed by WeChat and used in their production app. There are multiple React Native wrappers for this native solution; most of them are already based on JSI and therefore support synchronous and super-fast access.

Like `AsyncStorage`, MMKV is a simple key/value store. This means complex objects must be serialized to JSON strings before they can be stored. The API is nearly as simple as `AsyncStorage`:

```
import { MMKV } from 'react-native-mmkv'
export const storage = new MMKV()
// set data
const jsonValue = JSON.stringify(value)
storage.set('@key', jsonValue)
// get data
const strValue = storage.getString('@key')
const jsonValue = strValue!= null ? JSON.parse(strValue)  : null
```

As you can see, thanks to JSI, the API is synchronous, so we don't need to work with async/await syntax. In the second line, you can see the initialization of the store. This is one advantage over `AsyncStorage` because you can work with multiple instances of MMKV stores.

While it is possible to encrypt data with MMKV, at the time of writing, there is no secure solution regarding how to handle the key. Therefore, I would only recommend using it to store non-sensitive data. This may change in the future.

MMKV can be used as a faster drop-in replacement for `AsyncStorage`. The only disadvantage MMKV has compared to `AsyncStorage` is that the React Native wrappers are not used that much at the time of writing. There are two well-maintained React Native MMKV mappers, so you should have a look at them when you consider using MMKV for your project. You can find more information about installation, usage, and APIs there. The first one is `react-native-mmkv`. It is a leaner project and comes with a simpler API. It's also much simpler to install. You can have a look at it here: `https://github.com/mrousavy/react-native-mmkv`. The second one is `react-native-mmkv-storage`. It provides more features, such as indexing and data life cycle methods, which can be very useful when it comes to locking and transactions. You can have a look at it here: `https://github.com/ammarahm-ed/react-native-mmkv-storage`.

Now that we've looked at `AsyncStorage` and MMKV, which handle very similar use cases, let's look at a solution that comes with some more features: SQLite.

Working with SQLite

Compared to `AsyncStorage` and MMKV, SQLite is not only a simple key/value store – it is a complete database engine that includes functionalities such as locking, transactions, and advanced querying.

However, this means you can't simply store your objects as serialized data. SQLite uses SQL queries and tables to store your data, which means you have to process your objects. To insert data, you must create a table with a column for each property and then insert every object with a SQL statement. Let's have a look at the following code:

```
import { QuickSQLite } from 'react-native-quick-sqlite';
const dbOpenResult = QuickSQLite.open('myDB', 'databases');
// set data
let { status, rowsAffected } = QuickSQLite.executeSql(
  'myDB',
  'UPDATE users SET name = ? where userId = ?',
  ['John', 1]
);
if (!status) {
  console.log(`Update affected ${rowsAffected} rows`);
}
// get data
let { status, rows } = QuickSQLite.executeSql(
  'myDB',
  'SELECT name FROM users'
);
if (!status) {
  rows.forEach((row) => {
    console.log(row);
  });
}
```

As you can see, it takes much more code to insert and query data. You need to create and execute SQL and process the data you get to have it in a format you can work with. This means that SQLite isn't as easy and fast to use as `AsyncStorage` and MMKV, but it comes with advanced querying features. This means that you can filter and search your data and even join different tables.

I would recommend using SQLite if you have very complex data structures, where you need to join and query different objects or tables a lot. I prefer simpler solutions for local data storage, but there are use cases where SQLite is the better fit.

Besides the higher complexity of using it, SQLite also adds some MB to your app size because it adds its SQLite database engine implementation to your app.

The most used React Native wrapper for SQLite is `react-native-sqlite-storage`. The API is simple, and it is used in a lot of projects. You can learn more about it at `https://github.com/andpor/react-native-sqlite-storage`.

Another solution is `react-native-quick-sqlite`. It is a relatively new library, but it is based on JSI and therefore up to five times as fast as other solutions. You can learn more about it at `https://github.com/ospfranco/react-native-quick-sqlite`.

Now that you've learned about the SQLite database engine, let's look at another use case. Sometimes, you have to store large amounts of data, which means you need direct access to the filesystem. This is what we'll explore next.

Using the filesystem with React Native

To store large amounts of data, it is always a good idea to create and store files. On iOS and Android, every app runs in a sandbox that no other app has access to. While that does not mean that all your files are secure – they can be retrieved by the user quite easily – it gives you at least some level of privacy regarding your data. However, this sandbox mode means that you cannot access the data of other apps.

To read and write data to your app's sandbox in React Native, you can use libraries such as `react-native-fs`. This library provides constants with the paths you have access to and lets you read and write files from the filesystem.

I recommend using this approach when you're synchronizing files from a server or writing large amounts of data. Most of the time, you can combine this approach with one of the previous approaches to store files locally and then store the path of the file in one of the other storage solutions.

If you want to find out more about filesystem access on React Native, please have a look at the documentation of `react-native-fs` at `https://github.com/itinance/react-native-fs`.

With that, we've covered the most common solutions for storing and accessing non-sensitive data. This is where you should store most of your data. However, some data contains sensitive information such as passwords or other user information. This data needs another level of protection. So, let's have a look at some storage solutions for sensitive information in React Native.

Storing sensitive data

When you store sensitive information on the device of a user, you should always think about how to secure it. Most of the time, this will be irrelevant, but when the user loses the device, you should make sure that their sensitive information is as secure as possible.

You will never be able to ensure 100% data security when you have no control over the device. However, we need to do the best we can to make it as hard as possible for that sensitive information to be retrieved.

The first thing you should consider is if it is necessary to persist the information. Information that is not there cannot be stolen. If you need to persist information, use secure storage. Android and iOS provide built-in solutions for securely storing data. React Native provides wrappers for these native built-in solutions. The following ones are well maintained and can be used with ease:

- `expo-secure-store`: Uses iOS Keychain and Android `SharedPreferences` combined with Keystore System. It provides an easy API and can store values up to 2,048 bytes in size. More information can be found at `https://docs.expo.dev/versions/latest/sdk/securestore/`.

- `react-native-sensitive-info`: This library is very well maintained and provides a lot of functionality. It also adds another layer of security, which protects your data even on rooted devices. It supports Android, iOS, and Windows. More information can be found at `https://mcodex.dev/react-native-sensitive-info/`.

- `react-native-keychain`: This is another well-maintained library with an easy API. It supports Android and iOS and encrypts data on all devices. More information can be found at `https://github.com/oblador/react-native-keychain`.

Again, even if these solutions are very good and secure, based on native implementations, there will never be 100% security for data. So, please only persist necessary.

Now that you learned about data storage solutions and the difference between sensitive and non-sensitive data, it's time to look at navigation in React Native apps.

Understanding navigation in React Native

React Native does not come with a built-in navigation solution. That's why we worked with a global state and simply switched components while navigating in our example app. While this works technically, it does not provide a great user experience.

Modern navigation solutions include performance optimization, animations, integration in global state management solutions, and much more. Before we dive deep into these solutions, let's see what navigation looks like on different platforms.

Navigating different platforms

If you open any iOS or Android app, you'll soon realize that navigation in an app is completely different from navigating the web in a browser. A browser navigates from page to page by replacing the old page with the new one. In addition to that, every page has a URL and can be accessed directly if it's typed in the browser's address bar.

In an iOS or Android app, navigation takes the form of a combination of different navigators. The page you navigate away from doesn't always get replaced by the new one. Multiple pages can be active at the same time.

Let's have a look at the most common navigation scenarios and navigators to handle these scenarios:

- **Stack navigator**: When navigating to a new page in a stack navigator, the new page is pushed on top of the old page. Nevertheless, the old page doesn't get unmounted. It continues to exist and if you leave the new page with a back button, you'll automatically navigate back to the old page. The new page gets *popped* from the so-called layer stack, and you'll find your old page in the same state you left it in. This also includes the scroll position.

- **Tab navigator**: A very popular navigator is the tab navigator. This navigator provides up to five tabs that can be selected via a tab bar. This tab bar contains text and/or icons and can be on the top or at the bottom of the screen. Every tab has a layer stack. This means you can navigate every tab separately. The state of the tabs does not reset when you select another tab. In most cases, you simply have multiple stack navigators in your tab navigator.

- **Switch navigator**: This navigator provides the same behavior as web navigation. When using this navigator, you'll replace an old page or layer stack with the new one. This means the old page or layer stack gets unmounted and removed from memory. If you navigate back, the old page or layer stack will have a complete clean restart, as if you haven't been there before.

Most apps combine these navigators to provide a great navigation experience to the user. Because this common navigation experience in mobile apps is so different from the web, you should always keep this in mind when planning a project for mobile and the web. You will learn more about this in *Chapter 10, Structuring Large-Scale, Multi-Platform Projects*.

Even though multiple community projects provide great support for navigation in React Native apps, such as react-native-navigation (supported by Wix; more information can be found at `https://wix.github.io/react-native-navigation/docs/before-you-start/`) and react-router/native (more information can be found at `https://v5.reactrouter.com/native/guides/quick-start`), we'll focus on react-navigation in this section. It is by far the most commonly used, most actively maintained, and most advanced navigation solution for React Native.

Working with React Navigation

To understand how React Navigation works, it's best to simply integrate it into our example project. We'll do two things here. First, we'll replace our global state navigation solution with a React Navigation Stack Navigator. Then, we'll add a Tab Navigator to create a second tab, which we'll use in the next chapter.

But before you can begin using React Navigation, you must install it. This process is easy – you just have to install the package and the dependencies via npm. This can be done with the `npm install @react-navigation/native react-native-screens react-native-safe-area-context` command. Since `react-native-screens` and `react-native-safe-area-context` have a native part, you'll have to install the iOS Podfiles with the `npx pod-install` command. After this, you'll have to create fresh builds to be able to use React Navigation. This can be done for iOS with `npx react-native run-ios`.

At the time of writing, some additional steps are necessary to get React Navigation to work on Android. Since this may change in the future, please have a look at the installation part of the official documentation at `https://reactnavigation.org/docs/getting-started/#installation`.

Now that have installed React Navigation, it's time to use it in our example project. First, we'll replace our global state-based navigation in `App.tsx` with a Stack Navigator. To use the Stack Navigator, we'll have to install it using the `npm install @react-navigation/native-stack` command. Then, we can start using it in our app:

```
const MainStack =
createNativeStackNavigator<MainStackParamList>();
const App = () => {
  return (
    <NavigationContainer>
      <MainStack.Navigator>
        <MainStack.Screen
          name="Home"
          component={Home}
          options={{title: 'Movie Genres'}}
        />
        <MainStack.Screen
          name="Genre"
          component={Genre}
          options={{title: 'Movies'}}
        />
        <MainStack.Screen
          name="Movie"
```

```
        component={Movie}
        options={(({route}) =>
        ({title: route.params.movie.title})}
      />
    </MainStack.Navigator>
  </NavigationContainer>
 );
};
```

As you can see, our `App.tsx` got a lot simpler. We can remove all the `useState` hooks and all the setter functions because React Navigation will handle all this. All we need to do is create a Stack Navigator with React Navigation's `createNativeStackNavigator` command and then return our Layer Stack in our return statement. Please note `<NavigationContainer />`, which is wrapping the entire application. This is necessary to be able to manage the navigation state and should usually wrap the root component.

Here, every screen has a name, a component, and some options. The name is also the key that the screen can be navigated to with. `component` is the component that should be mounted when the screen is navigated to. `options` allows us to configure things such as the header and the back button.

Now that we have defined the Layer Stack, it's time to look at the views and see what has changed there. Let's look at `<GenreView />`. This is where we can see all the changes best:

```
type GenreProps = NativeStackScreenProps<MainStackParamList,
'Genre'>;
const Genre = (props: GenreProps) => {
  const [movies, setMovies] = useState<IMovie[]>([]);
  useEffect(() => {
    if (typeof props.route.params.genre !== 'undefined') {
      setMovies(getMovieByGenreId(props.route.params.genre.
        id));
    }
  }, [props.route.params.genre]);
  return (
    <ScrollContainer>
      {movies.map(movie => {
        return (
          <Pressable
            onPress={() =>
              props.navigation.navigate('Movie',
```

```
                        {movie: movie}) }>
              <Text
                style={styles.movieTitle}>{movie.title}</Text>
            </Pressable>
          );
        })}
      </ScrollContainer>
    );
  };
```

The first thing you can see is that there is another way to access the properties that are passed via React Navigation. Every component, which is a React Navigation screen, is passed two additional properties – `navigation` and `route`.

`route` contains information about the current route. The most important property of `route` is `params`. When navigating to a screen, we can pass `params`, which can then be retrieved through `route.params`. In this example, this is how we pass the genre to the view (`props.route.params.genre`), which we then use to fetch the movie list.

When you have a look at the `onPress` function of the `<Pressable />` component in the return statement, you can see how to navigate to another page in React Navigation. The `navigation` property provides different functions to navigate between screens. In our case, we use the `navigate` function with the `Movie` key to navigate to the `<Movie />` view. We also pass the current movie as a parameter.

When you compare the code to the example from the previous section, you'll realize that the `<Header />` and `<BackButton />` components are missing. This is because React Navigation comes with built-in header and back button support. While you can disable this, its default behavior is for every screen to have a header, including a back button to the previous screen.

If you want to see all these changes, please have a look at the repository for this example project and choose the `chapter-4-navigation` tag.

If you run the example project on that tag, you'll also see that React Native added animations to the navigation actions. These animations can be customized in any way possible. There is even a community library to support shared animated elements between the different pages. You can have a look at it here: `https://github.com/IjzerenHein/react-navigation-shared-element`.

Now that you've learned how to use the Stack Navigator, we'll add another navigator. We want to create a second tab because we want to create an area where the user can save his favorite movies. This will be done with a Tab Navigator.

As with the Stack Navigator, we have to install the Tab Navigator before using it. This can be done with npm `install @react-navigation/bottom-tabs`. After we have installed the Tab Navigator, we can add it to our `App.tsx`. Please have a look at the following code snippet:

```
const MainStackScreen = () => {
  return (
    <MainStack.Navigator>
      <MainStack.Screen component={Home}/>
      <MainStack.Screen component={Genre}/>
      <MainStack.Screen component={Movie}/>
    </MainStack.Navigator>
  );
};
const App = () => {
  return (
    <NavigationContainer>
      <TabNavigator.Navigator>
        <TabNavigator.Screen
          name="Main"
          component={MainStackScreen}
          options={{
            headerShown: false,
          }}
        />
        <TabNavigator.Screen
          name="User"
          component={User}
        />
      </TabNavigator.Navigator>
    </NavigationContainer>
  );
```

This is a very limited example. To see the working code, please have a look at the example repository and choose the `chapter-4-navigation-tabs` tag. As you can see, we move the Main Stack to its own function component. Our App component now contains `<TabNavigator />` with two screens.

The first screen gets `<MainStackScreen />` as its component. This means that we use our Stack Navigator when we are on the first tab. The second screen gets a newly created `<User />` component. You can switch between these tabs with the tab bar, which is created automatically by React Navigation.

> **Note**
>
> You should always install an icon library such as `react-native-vector-icons` (`https://github.com/oblador/react-native-vector-icons`) when working with tabs. Such libraries make it easy to find and use expressive icons for your tab bar.

This example, which contains two different navigators, shows the flexibility of React Navigation. We can either use our views in our `<Navigator.Screen />` components or use other navigators. This navigator nesting gives us nearly endless possibilities. Please note that in this case, we must hide the header for the first tab because it has already been created by our Stack Navigator. We can do this with the `headerShown: false` option.

As you can see, navigating with React Navigation is easy and powerful. It also has excellent TypeScript support, as you can see in the repository. You can create types for every layer stack and define exactly what can be passed to the different screens. This includes not only type checking, but also autocomplete functionality in most modern IDEs. You can read more about TypeScript support for React Navigation here: `https://reactnavigation.org/docs/typescript/`.

React Navigation supports a lot more features, including deeplinking, testing, persisting the navigation state, and integrating different state management solutions. If you want to learn more, please visit the official documentation: `https://reactnavigation.org/docs/getting-started/`.

Summary

Now that we've added a modern navigation library to our example project, it's time to wrap up this chapter. First, you learned what you have to consider when you wish to style your application. You also learned about the most common solutions for styling React Native applications and learned which of them are suitable for sharing code with web projects.

Then, you learned how to store data locally in a React Native app. Finally, you learned how navigation is different between the web and mobile and how to use a modern navigation library to implement state-of-the-art navigation solutions in React Native apps.

In the next chapter, we'll look at solutions for creating and maintaining a global app state and how to fetch data from external resources. While learning about this, we'll fill the placeholder screen we created in this chapter with some cool functionality.

5
Managing States and Connecting Backends

In the previous chapter, you learned how to build an app that works fine and looks great. In this chapter, we will focus on data. First, you will learn how to handle more complex data in your app. Then, you'll learn about different options regarding how to make your app communicate with the rest of the world by connecting it to remote backends.

In this chapter, we will cover the following topics:

- Managing global application states
- Working with global state management solutions
- Connecting to remote backends

Technical requirements

To be able to run the code in this chapter, you must set up the following:

- A working React Native environment (`bit.ly/prn-setup-rn` – React Native CLI Quickstart).
- While most of this chapter should also work on Windows, I recommend working on a Mac.
- To check out the simple examples, you can use `https://codesandbox.io/` and import `react-native-web` as a dependency. This provides all React Native components and transforms them into HTML tags.

Managing global application states

Since React Native is based on React, managing the application state does not differ much from React applications. There are dozens of well-maintained and working state management libraries available, all of which you can use in React Native. However, having a good plan and knowing how to manage the application state is much more important in an app than in a web application.

While it might be acceptable to wait a couple of seconds for data to appear or for a new page to load, this is not the case in a mobile app. Users are used to seeing information or changes immediately. So, you have to ensure that this also is the case in your app.

In this section, we'll have a look at the most popular state management solutions, but first, you'll learn about the different state management patterns and which one you should use for your project.

Passing properties

While it may work fine to only work with local component states in small applications and example projects, this approach is very limited. There are a lot of use cases where you have to share data between different components. The bigger your application grows, the more components you will have, and the more layers you will have to pass your data through.

The following diagram shows the main problem:

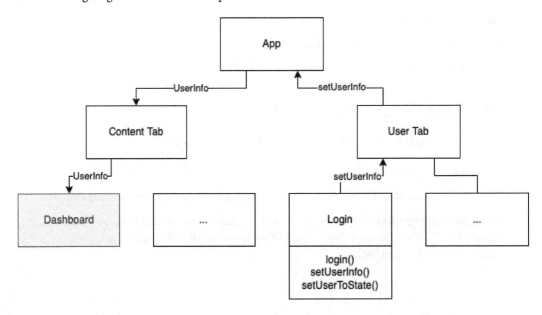

Figure 5.1 – State management without a global state management solution

The preceding diagram shows a very simple example that's very close to our example app, but you can already see the main problem: the app contains two tabs, one to show content and one to provide an individual user area. This second tab contains a login functionality, which is extracted in a login component.

The **Content** tab contains a dashboard component, which is mainly for showing content. But we also want to be able to adapt this content to the user. So, we need the information about the user in the dashboard component.

Without a global application state management library, we will have to do the following if a user logs in:

1. Pass the information from the **Login** component to the **User** tab.
2. Pass the information from the **User** tab to App.js.
3. Set the user information in the state of App.js.
4. Pass the user information as a prop to the **Content** tab.
5. Pass the user information from the **Content** tab to the **Dashboard** component.

Even in this simple example, we had to include five components to provide the user information to the dashboard component. When we are talking about complex real-world applications, there could be 10 or more layers that you would have to pass your data through. This would be a nightmare to maintain and understand.

There is another problem with this approach: when we pass the user information as a prop to the **Content** tab, this will re-render the whole **Content** tab if the user information in the state of App.js changes. This means that we re-render the **Content** tab and potentially a lot of child components that haven't changed because of the changed prop.

This is especially important because the global state of large apps can become quite complex and huge. If you compare this to a backend application, you can think of the global application state as the database of the system.

So, global state management libraries should solve two problems. On the one hand, they should give us an option to share information between components and keep our application's state management maintainable. On the other hand, they should also help reduce unnecessary re-renders and therefore optimize our app's performance.

Using global state providers/containers

The following diagram shows how the data flow is expected to work with a global state management solution:

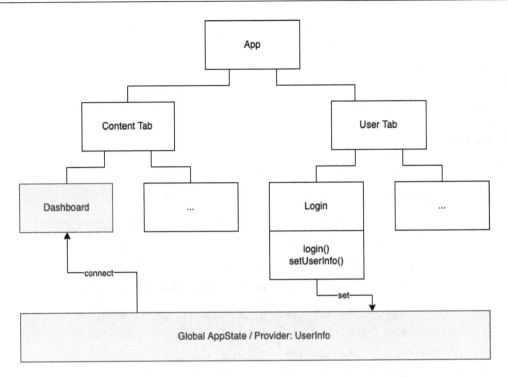

Figure 5.2 – State management with a global state management solution

As you can see, the global app state management solution provides an option to set data to a global place and connect components to consume this data. While this ensures that the connected components get re-rendered automatically when this data changes, it also has to guarantee that only these components are re-rendered and not the whole component tree.

While this is a good pattern, it also comes with some risks. When every component can connect to your global state, you have to be very careful in which ways this state can be edited.

> **Important note**
> Never allow any component to write directly to your state. No matter what library you use, your global state provider should always have control over how the state can be altered.

As mentioned in the preceding information box, your global state provider should always be in control of the state. This means that you should never allow any component to set the state directly. Instead, your app state provider should provide some functions that alter the state. This ensures that you always know in which ways your state can change. A state that can only be altered in these ways is also called a predictable state.

Using the predictable state pattern

Having a predictable state is especially important when working on large-scale projects with multiple developers. Imagine a project where anyone could simply set the state directly from any component. When you run into an error because your state contains an invalid value, which cannot be handled by your application, it is nearly impossible to find out where this value is coming from. Also, you cannot provide any central validation when you allow your state to be edited directly from outside the global state provider.

When you use the predictable state pattern, you have three advantages. First, you can provide validation and prevent invalid values from getting written to your state. Second, if you run into an error because of invalid state values, you have a central point where you can start debugging. Third, it's easier to write tests for it.

The pattern of creating a predictable state is shown in the following diagram:

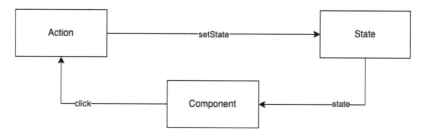

Figure 5.3 – Simple predictable state management

As you can see, a component triggers any event. In this example, a user clicks a button. This event triggers an action. This can be a custom Hook or a function that is provided by some state management library. This Hook or function can do multiple things, from validating the event to fetching data from a local storage solution or an external backend. In the end, the state will be set.

To give you a better idea, let's have a look at a concrete example. The component is a reload button. Upon clicking it, the action fetches the most recent data from the backend. It handles the request and if the request is successful and provides valid data, the action sets this data in the state. Otherwise, it sets an error message and provides code to the state.

As you can see, this pattern can also provide a good layer of abstraction between business logic and UI. If you would like to have an even better abstraction, you could use the next pattern we'll talk about.

Using the state/action/reducer pattern

This simple predictable state management pattern can be extended. The following diagram shows an extended version, which adds reducers and selectors:

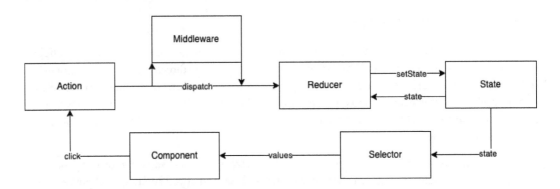

Figure 5.4 – The state/action/reducer pattern

The preceding diagram shows the so-called **state/action/reducer** pattern. In this pattern, the action is not a function or Hook but a JavaScript object that gets dispatched. In most cases, this action is handled by a reducer. The reducer takes the action, which can have some data as a payload, and processes it. It can validate data, merge the data with the current state, and set the state.

Normally, in this pattern, the reducer does not reach out to any other data sources. It only knows the action and the state. If you want to fetch data in this pattern, you can use middleware. This middleware intercepts the dispatched actions, processes its tasks, and dispatches other actions, which are then handled by reducers.

Again, let's have a look at a concrete example. A user clicks on the **Reload** button. This click dispatches a FETCH_DATA action. This FETCH_DATA action is handled by the middleware. The middleware fetches the data and validates the request. If everything worked fine, it dispatches a SET_DATA action with the new data as a payload.

The reducer handles this SET_DATA action, maybe does some data validation, merges the data with the current state, and sets the new state. If the data fetching in the middleware fails, the middleware dispatches a DATA_FETCH_ERROR action with an error code and error message as a payload. This action is also handled by a reducer, which sets the error code and message for the state.

Another difference between *Figure 5.3* and *Figure 5.4* is the existence of selectors. This is something that exists in different state management solutions because it makes it possible to subscribe to only a part of the state instead of the whole state. This is very useful because it makes it possible to create complex state objects while not always re-rendering your whole application.

This is clearer when we look at an example. Let's say that you have an application whose global state consists of a user, an array of articles, and an array of favorite article IDs. Your application shows the articles in one tab and every article has a button to add it to a favorite list. On a second tab, you show the user information.

When you put all this in the same global state, without using selectors, the default behavior of your **User** tab would be to re-render if you favor an article, even if nothing on the user page has changed. This is because the **User** tab also consumes the whole state and this state changed. When using a selector on the user, it doesn't re-render, because the user part of the state that the **User** tab is connected to didn't change.

If you were to use a complex state without selectors, you would have to create different state providers, which are completely independent of each other.

Now that you've learned about the different options, it's time to have a look at when it is necessary to use a global state or when you can also use a local component state and simply pass the props.

Comparing local component state and global application state

If you want to provide some data to be shown in your UI, you must store it in your state in most scenarios. But the interesting question is: In which state? Local component state or global application state?

This is a topic that has no simple answer or rules that fit every situation. However, I want to give you some guidelines so that you can make a good decision for all of your use cases:

- **Keep your global state as lean as possible**: Global variables are something that is very uncommon to use in most programming languages. And this is for a reason. If everything can be set anywhere in your application, it is hard to debug and maintain it. Also, the bigger the global application state grows, the more likely it is that you will run into performance problems.

- **Form data should not be part of the global state**: When you provide input fields such as text fields, toggles, date pickers, or anything else, the state of these components should not be part of the global application state. This information belongs to the view, which provides these fields and should therefore be part of the view's component state.

- **Try not to pass data down more than three layers**: When passing props to a child component, you should try to avoid passing this data through multiple layers. The best practice would be to never pass the component props to a child component, but only the component's state. However, this can be quite hard in practice, so I would recommend sticking to never passing data down more than three layers.

- **Try not to pass data up multiple layers**: As you have already learned, it is possible to pass data from a child to a parent component by passing a function from the parent to the child, which sets the state of the parent and then calls this function from the child component. Since this can lead to very confusing component dependencies to each other, you should be even more careful with passing data up than passing it down. I would recommend passing data up only one layer.

- **Use the global application state for data, which is used in multiple areas of your app**: When data has to be available in multiple areas of your app, which are on completely different navigation stacks, you should always use the global app state.

Deciding which data belongs to which state can be challenging. It is always a case-by-case decision and sometimes, you will have to revert your decision because of changing requirements or because you realize that it wasn't the right decision while working with it. That's fine. However, you can reduce these efforts by thinking about the right state solution for your data at the beginning.

Now that we've covered the theory, it's time to look at the most popular solutions and how to maintain the global application state.

Working with global state management solutions

Historically, we would have to start with Redux since it was the first global state management solution to be popular. Back in 2015, when it was introduced, it quickly became the de facto standard for global state management in React applications. It is still used very widely, but especially in the last 3 years, some other third-party solutions have emerged.

React also introduced a built-in solution for global state management that can be used in class components, as well as function components. It's called **React Context**, and since it ships with React, we'll start by looking at it.

Working with React Context

The idea of React Context is very simple: it is like a tunnel into a component that any other component can connect to. A context always consists of a provider and a consumer. The provider can be added to any existing component and expects a value property to be passed. All components that are descendants of the provider component can then implement a consumer and consume this value.

Working with plain React Context providers and consumers

The following code shows a plain React Context example:

```
export function App() {
  return (
    <ColorsProvider>
      <ColoredButton />
    </ColorsProvider>
  );
}
```

In your App.js file, you add a ColorsProvider, which wraps a ColoredButton component. This means that in ColoredButton, we will be able to implement a consumer for the ColorsProvider value. But let's have a look at the implementation of ColorsProvider first:

```
import defaultColors from "defaultColors";
export const ColorContext = React.createContext();
export function ColorsProvider(props) {
  const [colors, setColors] =
      useState(defaultColors.light);
  const toggleColors = () => {
    setColors((curColors) =>
        curColors === defaultColors.dark ?
            defaultColors.light : defaultColors.dark
    );
  };
  const value = {
    colors: colors,
    toggleColors: toggleColors
  };
  return <ColorContext.Provider value={value} {...props} />;
}
```

In this example, ColorsProvider is a function component that provides a state with the property colors. This is initialized with a default color scheme, which is imported from defaultColors. It also provides a toggleColors function, which changes the color schemes.

The colors state variable and the toggleColors function are then packed into a value object, which is passed to the value property of ColorContext.Provider. ColorContext is initialized in line 2.

As you can see, the file has two exports: ColorContext itself and the ColorsProvider function component. You have already learned how to use the provider, so next, we'll look at how to consume the context's value.

> **Note**
>
> The ColorsProvider function component isn't necessary for React Context to work. We could have also added the React Context initialization, the colors state, and the toggleColors function, as well as ColorContext.Provider directly into the App.js file. But it is best practice, and I would recommend extracting your contexts into separate files.

The following code shows `ColoredButton`, which is wrapped by our `ColorsProvider` in our `App.js` file:

```
function ColoredButton(props) {
    return (
        <ColorContext.Consumer>
            {(({ colors, toggleColors }) => {
                return (
                    <Pressable
                        onPress={toggleColors}
                      style={{
                          backgroundColor: colors ?
                          colors.background :
                          defaultColors.background
                      }}
                    >
                      <Text
                          style={{
                              color: colors ? colors.foreground :
                              defaultColors.foreground
                          }}
                      >
                          Toggle Colors
                      </Text>
                    </Pressable>
                );
            }}
        </ColorContext.Consumer>
    );
}
```

As you can see, we use a `ColorContext.Consumer` component, which provides the values of `ColorsProvider`. These values can then be used. In this case, we use the `colors` object to style the `Pressable` and `Text` components and we pass the `toggleColors` function to the `onPress` property of the `Pressable` component.

This method of implementing a consumer works in function components as well as in class components. When working with function components, there is a simpler syntax you can use to fetch the value of the context.

Working with Context and React Hooks

The following code example shows a small section of the code example we looked at previously:

```
function ColoredButton(props) {
const {colors, toggleColors} = React.useContext(ColorContext);
   return (
           <Pressable
               onPress={toggleColors}
```

As you can see, instead of having to implement the context consumer component, you can simply use the useContext Hook to fetch the values. This makes the code shorter and much more readable.

While this example is very simple, it nevertheless follows best practices. As you can see, the setColors function, which is the setter for our state, isn't publicly available. Instead, we provide a toggleColors function, which allows us to alter the state in a predefined way. Also, we have the state abstracted very well from the UI.

Hooks enable you to even go one step further. When the project grows and you want to have an additional layer of abstraction, such as for making external requests, you could create a custom Hook as your middleware.

This is what we will add next to our example project. We'll create some functionality so that the user can create a list of favorite movies, which then gets displayed in the **User** tab. While doing this, we'll discuss the benefits and limitations of React Context for global state management.

The following figure shows what we'll create:

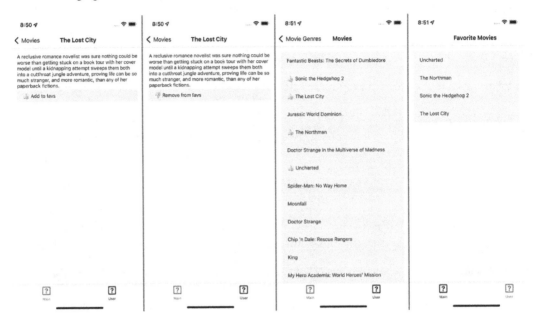

Figure 5.5 – Example app – Favorite Movies

This is what the app should be able to do. On each movie details page, we'll add a button to add the movie to **Favorite Movies**. If a movie is already part of **Favorite Movies**, the button changes to a **Remove** button, which removes the movie from the list.

In the **Movies** list, we want to add a thumbs-up icon to all movies that are part of the **Favorite Movies** list. Finally, we want to display all movies in the **User** tab.

First, we have to create the context and the custom Hook to be able to store the data. The following code shows `UserProvider`:

```
export function UserProvider(props: any) {
  const [name, setName] = useState<string>('John');
  const [favs, setFavs] = useState<{ [favId: number]:
      IMovie}>({});
  const addFav = (fav: IMovie): void => {
    if (!favs[fav.id]) {
      const _favs = {...favs};
      _favs[fav.id] = fav;
      setFavs(_favs);
```

```
        }
    };
    const removeFav = (favId: number): void => {
        if (favs[favId]) {
            const _favs = {...favs};
            delete _favs[favId];
            setFavs(_favs);
        }
    };
    const value = {
        name, favs, addFav, removeFav,
    };
    return <UserContext.Provider value={value} {...props} />;
}
```

As you can see, we have two state variables: an object that stores the favorite movies in a map-like structure (favs) and the name of the user (name). You can ignore name for now; we'll need this later.

The provider also contains addFav and removeFav functions, which are the only ways to edit the store from outside the provider. These two functions and the name and favs state variables are packed into the value variable, which then gets passed to the value property of the provider.

Next, we'll have a look at the custom Hook. This Hook serves as the middleware and the data selectors. It is used to fetch data before it's stored and to transform data to provide it in the way it is needed:

```
export function useUser() {
    const context = React.useContext(UserContext);
    const {name, favs, addFav, removeFav} = context;
    const addFavById = (favId: number): void => {
        const movie = getMovieById(favId);
        if (!movie) {
            return;
        }
        addFav(movie);
    };
    const getFavsAsArray = (): IMovie[] => {
        return Object.values(favs);
    };
    const isFav = (favId: number): boolean => {
```

```
        return !!favs[favId];
    };
    return {
        name, favs, getFavsAsArray, removeFav, addFavById,
        isFav,
    };
}
```

As we did in our previous Hooks example, we'll use the `useContext` Hook to make the provider's data accessible in our custom Hook. The custom Hook contains three functions. The `addFavById` function takes a `movieId` and fetches the movie from our `movieService`. This is a typical middleware task.

The `getFavsAsArray` function provides the favorite movies of a user as an array. The `isFav` function answers the question if a given ID belongs to a movie in the user's favorite list. These two functions are typical selectors.

The Hook returns these three functions as well as `name`, `favs`, and `removeFav` from the provider. With these things, we have all we need to implement our requirements very easily.

Let's start with the movie details page. We'll have a look at different parts of the added code; if you want to see the whole file, please visit this book's GitHub repository:

```
const Movie = (props: MovieProps) => {
  const {isFav, addFavById, removeFav} = useUser();
  const _isFav = isFav(props.route.params.movie.id);
  ...
```

In this component, we need the `isFav` function to check if a movie is already part of the user's favorites. Depending on that, we want to be able to add or remove the movie to or from the user's favorites. Therefore, we import our `useUser` Hook and then use object destructuring to make these functions available. We also store the `isFav` information in a variable for later use.

Now that we can work with these functions, we have to implement the button itself:

```
<Pressable
  style={styles.pressableContainer}
  onPress={
    _isFav
      ? () => removeFav(props.route.params.movie.id)
      : () => addFavById(props.route.params.movie.id)
  }>
```

```
    <Text style={styles.pressableText}>
        {_isFav ? '🖓 Remove from favs' : '👍 Add to favs'}
    </Text>
</Pressable>
```

As you can see, the implementation part of the button is quite easy. We use our _isFav variable to check which text our button should display and to decide which function we should call. The addFavById and removeFav functions can be called like any other function provided by the component.

Now that we have built the functionality to edit the favorites, the next step is to display this information in the movies list. The import of the Hook works as follows in the movie details view:

```
const Genre = (props: GenreProps) => {
    const [movies, setMovies] = useState<IMovie[]>([]);
    const {isMovieFav} = useUser();
    ...
```

Since we don't want to write anything to the state, we don't need to make these functions available. And in contrast to the movie details page, we must check multiple movies for their favorite status, so it makes no sense to create a variable to cache the result of isMovieFav here.

Next, let's look at the implementation of the movie list's JSX:

```
    return (
        <ScrollContainer>
            {movies.map(movie => (
                <Pressable
                    {isMovieFav(movie.id) ? (
                        <Text style={styles.movieTitleFav}>👍</Text>
                    ) : undefined}
                    <Text style={styles.movieTitle}>{movie.title}
                    </Text>
                </Pressable>
            ))}
        </ScrollContainer>
    );
```

While iterating over the movies, we'll check every movie with the isMovieFav function. If it returns true, we'll add a thumbs-up icon. That's the only change that is needed here.

The last step is to show the list of **Favorite Movies** in the **User** tab. This is also just a few lines of code:

```
const User = (props: UserProps) => {

  const {getMovieFavsAsArray} = useUser();
  const _movieFavsArray = getMovieFavsAsArray();
  return (
    <ScrollContainer>
      {_movieFavsArray.map(movie => {
        return (
          <Pressable>
            <Text style={styles.movieTitle}>{movie.title}
            </Text>
          </Pressable>
        );
      })}
    </ScrollContainer>
  );
};
```

The preceding code shows the whole component (except imports and styling). We fetch our favorite movies with the Hook's getMovieFavsAsArray function and store them in a variable. Then, we iterate over the array and render the movies. That's it! Our example is complete.

As you have seen in this example, the implementation part of the components is very easy and only needs a few lines of code in most cases. This will stay the same, even in bigger projects, when you have a good structure in your contexts. I like this approach very much because it doesn't need any external libraries and has a clear separation between UI components, middleware, and state provider. It also comes with another benefit.

It can be very useful to persist parts of the store and rehydrate (reload) them when the user reopens the app. This is also very easy when working with React Context. The following code snippet is part of UserProvider and shows how to store and reload the user's favorite list.

In this case, we are using AsyncStorage as a local storage solution:

```
useEffect(() => {
  AsyncStorage.getItem('HYDRATE::FAVORITE_MOVIES').then
    (value => {
      if (value) {
        setFavs(JSON.parse(value));
```

```
            }
        });
    }, []);
    useEffect(() => {
        if (favs !== {}) {
            AsyncStorage.setItem('HYDRATE::FAVORITE_MOVIES',
                JSON.stringify(favs));
        }
    }, [favs]);
```

Since the provider works like any other component, it can also use the useEffect Hook. In this example, we are using an effect to fetch favs from AsyncStorage when the provider gets mounted. We use another effect to store the favorites every time the favs variable changes. While there are a lot of benefits, unfortunately, this approach based on React Context comes with a big limitation.

Understanding the limitations of React Context

At the beginning of this example, I told you to ignore the name variable in the state provider because we would need it later. This later is now. If you have already looked at this book's GitHub repository, you may have realized that the code for the Home view has changed.

The following code snippet shows the changes:

```
const Home = (props: HomeProps) => {
    const {name} = useUser();
    ...
    console.log('re-render home');
    return (
        <ScrollContainer>
            <Text style={styles.welcome}>Hello {name}</Text>
    ...
```

This view now imports the useUser Hook and reads the user's name to provide a warm welcome message to the user. It also contains a console.log that logs every re-render of the page. When you run the code example and add/remove movies to/from the user's favorites, you'll realize that the Home component re-renders on every change of favs in UserProvider.

This happens even if we don't use favs in this component. This is because a state change in UserProvider triggers a re-render in every descendant, which also contains every component that imports the custom Hook.

This limitation does not mean that you can't use React Context. It is widely used, even in large projects. But you always have to keep this limitation in mind. My recommended solution for this problem is to split your global state into different contexts with different providers.

In this example, we could have created a `UserContext`, which only contains the name of the user, and a `FavContext`, which only contains the list of favorites.

You could also use `useMemo`, `React.memo`, or `componentDidUpdate` to optimize the performance of this approach. But if you need to do this, I recommend using another solution that provides these optimizations out of the box. One of them is Zustand, which we'll have a look at next.

Working with Zustand

Zustand.js is a very lean approach to state management. It is based on Hooks and comes with performance-optimized selectors built in. It can also be extended in different ways so that you can use it to implement exactly the global state management pattern you like.

> **Note**
> If you want to use Zustand in class components, you can't do this directly because class components don't support Hooks. However, you could use the **higher-order component (HOC)** pattern to wrap the class component in a function component. Then, you can use the Hook in the function component and pass the Zustand state to the class component as a prop.
>
> You can read more about HOC in the React documentation here: `https://bit.ly/ prn-hoc`.

To create a Zustand store, you must use the `create` Hook provided by Zustand. This creates a store, which holds the state and provides functions to access the state. To get a more concrete idea, let's have a look at what our example project looks like with the global state handled by Zustand.

The code snippets shown here are just excerpts. If you want to check out the running example, please go to this book's GitHub repository and choose the `chapter-5-zustand` tag:

```
export const useUserStore = create<IUser &
UserStoreFunctions>((set, get) => ({
  name: 'John',
  favs: {},
  addFavById: (favId: number) => {
    const _favs = {...get().favs};
    if (!_favs[favId]) {
      const movie = getMovieById(favId);
      if (movie) {
```

```
        _favs[favId] = movie;
        set({favs: _favs});
      }
    }
  },
  removeFav: (favId: number) => {
    const _favs = {...get().favs};
    if (_favs[favId]) {
      delete _favs[favId];
      set({favs: _favs});
    }
  },
}));
```

We use the create function provided by Zustand to create the store. We pass a function to create that can access the get and set parameters and returns the store. This store itself is an object that can hold data objects (the state) and functions (setters or selectors) as properties. Inside these functions, we can use get to access state objects or set to write parts of the store.

Again, when you work with objects as part of your state, you have to create a new object and write it to the store to trigger a re-render. If you just alter the existing state object and write it back, the state will not be recognized as changed because the object reference did not change.

> **Tip**
>
> When working with objects in your state, it can be annoying to always have to create copies of these objects before setting them to the state. This problem is solved by an open source library called **immer.js**. This library provides a produce function, which takes the old state, lets you make changes, and automatically creates a new object out of it. It also integrates into Zustand as middleware.
>
> You can find out more about immer.js here: https://bit.ly/prn-immer.

In our example, we still have name and favs as state properties. To modify this state, our Zustand store provides an addFavById function and a removeFav function. The addFavById function not only writes to the store but also fetches the movie for a given ID from our movieService.

Next, we'll look at how we connect to the store from within a component. We don't even have to change much code to switch from React Context to Zustand in our components.

Let's have a look at the movie view:

```
const Movie = (props: MovieProps) => {
  const [addFavById, favs, removeFav] = useUserStore(state
      => [
          state.addFavById,
          state.favs,
          state.removeFav,
        ], shallow);
  const _isFav = favs[props.route.params.movie.id];
  ...
```

Here, we use the useUserStore Hook we just created with Zustand's create function to connect to the Zustand state. We connect to multiple parts of the state using array destructuring. Since we have already implemented the usage of the functions in our JSX code in the React Context example, we don't have to change anything there. It's the same functions doing the same thing, but coming from another state management solution.

However, the most important thing occurs when looking at the Home view:

```
const Home = (props: HomeProps) => {
  const name = useUserStore(state => state.name);
  console.log('rerender home');
  ...
```

Here, we are doing the same as we did in the React Context example: we are connecting our home view to the global state and fetching the name. When you run this example, you will realize that console.log will no longer be triggered when you add or remove favorites.

This is because Zustand only triggers re-renders if the part of the state the component is connected to changes, not if anything in the state changes. This is very useful because you don't have to think about performance optimization that much. Zustand provides this out of the box.

Zustand is becoming more and more popular because of its simplicity and flexibility. As mentioned previously, you don't have to choose this simple approach with Zustand. You could even create a Redux-like workflow with it.

Speaking of Redux, this is the next solution you'll learn about.

Working with Redux

Redux is by far the most used solution when it comes to global state management. The following diagram compares the usage of react-redux and Zustand:

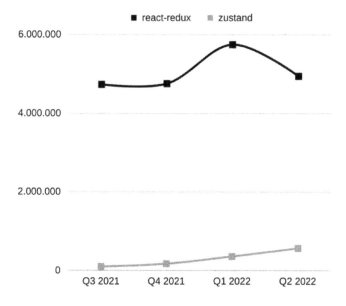

Figure 5.6 – Daily npm downloads of react-redux and Zustand

As you can see, the daily downloads of react-redux are quite stable at around 5 million. Zustand's popularity is rapidly growing. It changed from around 100,000 daily downloads in Q3 2021 to around 500,000 daily downloads in Q2 2022. This is a sign that a lot of new projects prefer Zustand over Redux.

Nevertheless, Redux is a very good solution. It follows a very clear structure and has a huge ecosystem built around it. Redux uses the state/action/reducer pattern and forces the developer to stick to it. It can be enhanced with different middlewares such as redux-thunk or redux-saga to handle effects. It also provides great developer tools for debugging.

Since Redux is a very mature technology, there are a lot of great tutorials and books on the market that handle Redux. Therefore, the basic usage of Redux won't be covered by this book. If you don't already know the basics of Redux, I recommend starting with the official tutorial here: https://bit.ly/prn-redux.

While Redux is a great state management solution, it comes with two huge downsides. First, it creates some overhead for creating and maintaining all the parts of the process. To provide a simple string value in your global state, you need at least the store, a reducer, and an action. Second, the code of applications with a deep Redux integration can become quite hard to read.

I would recommend Redux for huge applications that a lot of developers work on. In this case, the clear structure and the separation between the logical layers are worth the overhead. Middleware should be used to handle side effects and `redux-toolkit` can be used to simplify the code. This setup can work very well in this large-scale scenario.

Now that you've learned how to use Redux, Zustand, and React Context to handle the global application state, you have seen that there are multiple different ways to approach global state management. While these solutions are my favorites at the moment, there are a lot more options available. If you want to look for different options, I also recommend MobX, MobX-state-tree, Recoil, and Rematch.

Now that you've learned how to handle data inside a React Native app, we'll check out how we can retrieve data from external APIs.

Connecting to remote backends

React Native allows you to use different solutions to connect to online resources such as APIs. First, you'll learn about plain HTTP API connections. Later in this section, we'll also have a look at more high-level solutions such as GraphQL clients and SDKs such as Firebase or Amplify. But let's start with some general things.

Understanding the general principles of connections in React Native

No matter what connection solution you use in your React Native app, it is always a good idea to use **JavaScript Object Notation (JSON)** as the format for your data transfer. Since React Native apps are written in JavaScript and JavaScript plays very well with JSON, this is the only logical choice.

Next, regardless of which connection solution you use, always wrap your API calls in a service. Even if you are sure about the connection solution you chose, you may want or have to replace it in a few years.

This is much simpler when you have all the code wrapped in a service than searching for it everywhere in your whole application. The last thing I want to mention here is that you have to think about how to secure your API.

Understanding security risks

You always have to keep in mind that a React Native app runs completely client-side. This means that everything you ship in your app can be considered publicly available. This also includes API keys, credentials, or any other authentication information. While there can never be 100% impenetrable software, you should at least provide some level of security:

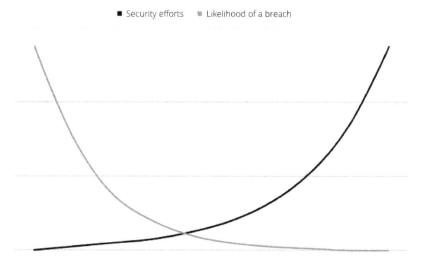

Figure 5.7 – Security efforts and likelihood of a breach (inspired by https://reactnative.dev/docs/security)

As you can see, even some efforts in securing your app reduce the likelihood of a breach significantly. The minimum you should do is as follows:

- Don't store your private API keys or credentials in your code.
- Don't use tools such as `react-native-dotenv` or `react-native-config` to store sensitive data. This data is also shipped to the client in plain text.
- Use user-based keys or credentials wherever possible.
- Remove all console output in production builds to not expose keys.
- Store sensitive information in secure local storage solutions (see the *Storage* section of *Chapter 4, Styling, Storage, and Navigation in React Native*).

When you need to work with third-party APIs, which only provide you with one key, you should create your own server layer that you can call from within your app. Then, you can store your API key on the server, add it to the request, call the third-party API from your server, and provide the response to your app.

In that way, you don't make your API key public. Again, always keep in mind that everything you ship with your app can be exposed.

With that warning given, let's start with our first simple call, where we will use the JavaScript Fetch API.

Working with the built-in Fetch API

React Native ships with a built-in Fetch API, which is sufficient for most use cases. It is easy to use, easy to read, and can be used in apps of all sizes. We'll use our example app again to see how it works. We'll replace the `genres.json` and `movies.json` static files with real API calls to The Movie DB (`https://www.themoviedb.org`). Please note that this API is free for non-commercial use only and you have to stick to the terms of use when using it.

You can find the full example code on GitHub (the `chapter-5-fetch` tag). To run it, you have to register at `https://www.themoviedb.org/` and obtain an API key. You can read more about this here: `https://bit.ly/prn-tmd-api`.

Now, let's have a look at the code. First, we must create a constants file for all API information:

```
export const APIConstants: {
  API_URL: string;
  API_KEY: string;
     } = {
          API_URL: 'https://api.themoviedb.org/3/',
          API_KEY: '<put your api key here - never do that
             in production>',
};
```

In our example, we put the base URL and the API key here. This is where you can paste the API key you retrieved from The Movie DB.

> **Security note**
> Never put your API key in your app like this in production.

Since we have already extracted our data connection in `movieService`, this is the file where we will make most of the changes. Instead of reading and filtering local files, we'll connect to the real API. To make the connection easier, we'll write two helper functions first:

```
const createFullAPIPath: (path: string) => string = path => {
  return (
    APIConstants.API_URL + path +
        (path.includes('?') ? '&' : '?') +
        'api_key=' + APIConstants.API_KEY
    );
};
```

```
async function makeAPICall<T>(path: string): Promise<T> {
  console.log(createFullAPIPath(path));
  const response = await fetch(createFullAPIPath(path));
  return response.json() as Promise<T>;
}
```

The `createFullAPIPath` function takes the path of the request and adds the base URL and the API key for authentication to the call. The `makeAPICall` function does the fetch action and returns typed data from the response JSON.

These helper functions are used to create different functions that are exported so that they're available in the application. Let's look at one of them – the `getGenres` function:

```
const getGenres = async (): Promise<Array<IGenre>> => {
  let data: Array<IGenre> = [];
  try {
    const apiResponse = await makeAPICall<{genres: Array
      <IGenre>}>('genre/movie/list',
    );
    data = apiResponse.genres;
  } catch (e) {
    console.log(e);
  }
  return data;
};
```

As you can see, we use the `makeAPICall` helper function to fetch the data. We add the data type we expect the data to be. As the path, we only have to pass the relative path of the API. Then, we process the response and return the data. In production, we wouldn't log the error to the console but to an external error reporting system. You'll learn more about this in *Chapter 13, Tips and Outlook*.

There is one simple thing left that we have to change in our application to make it work again. You may have noticed that the functions in our service changed to `async` functions, which return promises instead of direct data. While we were able to process the local data synchronously, API calls are always executed asynchronously.

And that's a good thing. You don't want your application to freeze until the response to your API request is there. But since the service function returns promises now, we have to modify the places where these functions are called.

So, let's have a look at the home view again – more precisely, the `useEffect` Hook part:

```
useEffect(() => {
  const fetchData = async () => {
    setGenres(await getGenres());
  };
  fetchData();
}, []);
```

Since we are not able to create async functions directly in the `useEffect` Hook, we create an async `fetchData` function that we then call in `useEffect`. In this function, we await the promise that is returned by `getGenres` and set the data in the state.

Similar changes have to be made in the `genre` view, the `movie` view, and the `addFavById` function of our Zustand store.

While Fetch is quite powerful and you can use it even in large-scale and enterprise projects, some other solutions can be useful too.

Working with other data fetching solutions

In this subsection, you'll learn about other popular solutions for data fetching. All of them have their benefits and tradeoffs and in the end, you have to decide what's the best fit for your project. The following solutions work fine, are well maintained, and are widely used:

- **Axios**: Axios is a third-party HTTP client for fetching data. It works quite similarly to the Fetch API but brings a lot of additional features. Once created, you can configure your Axios instance with headers, interceptors, and more. It also provides excellent error handling and allows you to cancel requests.

- **Apollo/URQL GraphQL client**: GraphQL is a query language for APIs that has become very popular over the last few years. The advantage it has over REST APIs is that you can control what you want to fetch on the client. You can also fetch multiple resources in one call. This results in fetching exactly the data you need in the most efficient way possible. You can read more about GraphQL here: `https://bit.ly/prn-advantage-graph`.

  There are multiple client implementations for GraphQL. The most popular ones are Apollo and URQL. Both clients not only provide data fetching but also handle caching, refreshing, and data actualization in the UI. While this can be very useful, you always should ensure that you also provide a great user experience for users while they are offline.

- **React Native Firebase**: Firebase is a very popular app development backend platform. It provides different services with very well-maintained SDKs. React Native Firebase is a wrapper around the native Android and iOS SDK. It provides data fetching, but only for connections to the Firebase services. If you want to learn more about Firebase, you can visit the React Native Firebase documentation: `https://bit.ly/prn-firebase`.

- **AWS Amplify**: Amplify is a collection of AWS services that can be accessed via the Amplify SDKs. Like Firebase, it provides data fetching capabilities, but only to the AWS services that have been configured in Amplify. If you want to learn more about Amplify, you can visit the Amplify JavaScript documentation: `https://bit.ly/prn-amplify`.

Besides these solutions, a lot of service providers provide their own SDKs that can be used to access their services. It is totally fine to use these SDKs. But again, always remember to not store any API keys or authentication information in your app.

Summary

To wrap this chapter up, let's have a short recap. In this chapter, you learned how to handle local and global states. You learned about the most popular concepts of global state handling and how to decide which data should be stored in your global state or the local state of a component or view. You also understood how to use React Context, Zustand, and Redux for global state handling.

After mastering state management in React Native, you learned how to connect your app to a remote backend. You understood how to use the built-in Fetch API, how to extract API calls in a service, how to create and use helper functions, and how to work with async calls. Finally, you learned about the different solutions for data fetching, such as Axios, GraphQL clients, and other SDKs.

Now that you have completed the first five chapters of this book, you can create a working app with a strong technical foundation. In the next chapter, you will learn how to make your app look good with beautiful animations.

6
Working with Animations

Animations are part of every mobile app. Smooth animations can make the difference between whether a user feels comfortable using an app or not. Essentially, an animation is just the screen rendering again and again, transitioning from one state to another.

This rendering should happen so quickly that the user doesn't realize the single states of the animation but perceives it as a smooth animation. To take this one step further, animations not only transform from state A to state B over time, but they also react to user interactions such as scrolling, pressing, or swiping.

Most devices have a screen frame rate of 60 **frames per second (fps)**, and modern devices already have 120 fps (at the time of writing, React Native only supports 60 fps, which you can learn about on GitHub at `bit.ly/prn-rn-fps`). This means that when running an animation, the screen has to be re-rendered at 60 fps.

This is quite challenging because calculating complex animations and re-rendering the screen are some of the most compute-intense operations. Especially on low-end devices, the computing of the animation can become too slow, and the screen refresh rate drops below 60/120 fps. This then makes the animation and the app feel sluggish and slow.

Essentially, you can group animations into two different types:

- **On-screen animations**: These animations only apply to a part of the screen. There are a lot of different use cases for this type of animation such as grabbing user attention, giving touch feedback, showing indications of progress or loading, or improving the scrolling experience.

- **Full-screen animations**: These animations transition the whole screen. Most of the time, this type of animation is used to navigate to another screen.

Since full-screen animations are handled internally by all popular navigation libraries, this chapter will focus on on-screen animations. Full-screen animations have been covered in the *Navigating in React Native apps* section of *Chapter 4, Styling, Storage, and Navigation, Section Navigation.*

There are multiple ways to achieve smooth animations in React Native. Depending on the type of project and animations you want to build, you can choose from a wide range of solutions, each with its own advantages and disadvantages. We will discuss the best and most widely used solutions in this chapter.

In this chapter, we will cover the following topics:

- Understanding the architectural challenge of animations in React Native
- Using the internal React Native Animated API
- Creating simple animations with `react-native-animatable`
- Exploring Reanimated 2 – the most complete animation framework for React Native
- Using Lottie animations in React Native

> **Info**
> There have been some interesting developments about using the Skia rendering engine (which powers Chrome, Firefox, Android, and Flutter) to render animations in React Native, but at the time of writing, this approach is not production ready.

Technical requirements

To be able to run the code in this chapter, you have to set up the following things:

- A working React Native environment (`bit.ly/prn-setup-rn` – React Native CLI Quickstart)
- An iOS/Android simulator or a real device (a real device is preferred)

Understanding the architectural challenge of animations in React Native

The current architecture of React Native is suboptimal when it comes to animations. Think of an animation that scales or moves a title image based on the vertical scroll value of a `ScrollView`; this animation has to be calculated based on the scroll value of the `ScrollView` and immediately re-render the image. The following diagram shows what would happen when using the plain React Native architecture:

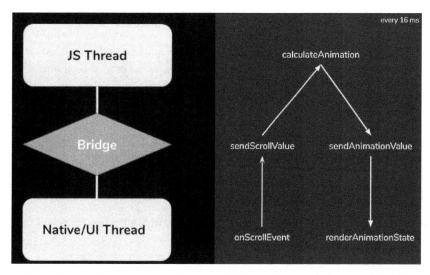

Figure 6.1 – The React Native architecture while animating based on scroll values

Here, you can see the general React Native architecture. The JavaScript thread is where you write your code. Every command will be serialized and sent via the bridge to the native thread. In this thread, the command is deserialized and executed. The same happens with the user input, but it occurs the other way around.

For our animation, this means that the scroll value would have to be serialized, sent via the bridge, deserialized, transferred via a complex calculation to an animation value, serialized, transferred back via the bridge, deserialized, and then rendered. This whole process has to be done every 16 milliseconds (or 60 times a second).

This round-trip leads to multiple problems:

- The serialization/deserialization process consumes unnecessary compute power
- In most cases, the calculation in JavaScript is slower than in native code
- The calculation can block the JavaScript thread and make the app unresponsive
- The round-trip can lead to frame drops and make the animation look sluggish and slow

Because of these problems, it is not a good idea to write animations in your own plain React Native code (for example, by setting a state in a loop). Fortunately, there are multiple production-ready solutions to avoid these problems and achieve high-quality animations.

In the following sections, we will have a look at four different solutions. Every solution has advantages and disadvantages, and which solution should be preferred depends on the project and the use case. Let's start with the built-in Animated API.

Using the internal Animated API of React Native

React Native comes with a built-in Animated API. This API is quite powerful, and you can achieve a lot of different animation goals with it. In this section, we will have a brief look at how it works and what advantages and limitations the internal Animated API has.

For a complete tutorial, please have a look at the official documentation at bit.ly/prn-animated-api.

To understand how the Animated API works, let's start with a simple example.

Starting with a simple example

The following code implements a simple fade-in animation, which makes a view appear over the duration of 2 seconds:

```
import React, { useRef } from "react";
import { Animated, View, Button } from "react-native";

const App = () => {
  const opacityValue = useRef(new Animated.Value(0)).
      current;
  const showView = () => {
    Animated.timing(opacityValue, {
        toValue: 1,
        duration: 2000
        }).start();
    };
  return (
    <>
      <Animated.View
        style={{
          backgroundColor: 'red',
            opacity: opacityValue
        }}
      />
      <Button title="Show View" onPress={showView} />
    </>
  );
```

```
}
export default App;
```

The Animated API is based on animated values. These values are changed over time and are used as part of the application styling. In this example, we initialize opacityValue as an Animated.Value component with the initial value of 0.

As you can see, the JSX code contains an Animated.View component whose style uses opacityValue as the opacity property. When running this code, the Animated.View component is completely hidden at the beginning; this is because the opacity is set to 0. When pressing the **Show View** button, showView is called, which starts an Animated.timing function.

This Animated.timing function expects an Animated.Value component as the first property and a config object as the second parameter. The Animated.Value component is the value that should be changed during the animation. With the config object, you can define the general conditions of the animation.

In this example, we want to change the Animated.Value component to 1 over the duration of 2 seconds (2,000 ms). Then, the Animated.timing function calculates the different states of the animation and takes care of the rendering of the Animated.View component.

> **Good to know**
>
> Essentially, you can animate every part of your UI. The Animated API exports some components directly, such as Animated.View, Animated.Image, Animated.ScrollView, Animated.Text, and Animated.FlatList. But you can animate any component by using Animated.createAnimatedComponent().

While the Animated API does not completely solve the problem of the React Native architecture, it is an improvement over just setting the state again and again and again, as it greatly reduces the payload that has to be transferred from the JavaScript thread to the native thread, but this transfer has to be done every frame. To prevent this transfer in every frame, you have to use the native driver, as shown in the following subsection.

Using the native driver

When configuring the animation with the config object, you can set a property called useNativeDriver. This is very important and should be done whenever possible.

When using the native driver with useNativeDriver: true, React Native sends everything to the native thread before starting the animation. This means that the animation runs completely on the native thread, which guarantees a smooth-running animation and no frame drops.

Unfortunately, the native driver is currently limited to non-layout properties. So, things such as transform and opacity can be used in an animation with the native driver, whereas all the Flexbox and position properties, such as `height`, `width`, `top`, or `left`, can't be used.

Interpolate animated values

In some cases, you don't want to use the `Animated.Value` component directly. This is where interpolation comes into play. Interpolation is a simple mapping of input and output ranges. In the following code example, you can see an interpolation, which adds a position change to the simple example from before:

```
style={{
    opacity: opacityValue,
    transform: [{
      translateY: opacityValue.interpolate({
        inputRange: [0, 1],
        outputRange: [50, 0]
      }),
    }],
  }}
```

In this code example, we added a transform `translateY` property to the `style` object. This property transforms the vertical position of an object. We don't set a fixed value, nor do we bind `opacityValue` directly.

We use an interpolate function with a defined `inputRange` value of `[0,1]` and a defined `outputRange` value of `[50,0]`. Essentially, this means that the `translateY` value will be 50 when `opacityValue` (which is our `AnimatedValue`) is 0 and will be 0 when `opacityValue` is 1. This results in our `AnimatedView` moving up 50px to its original position while fading in.

> **Tip**
> Try to use interpolation to reduce the number of animated values you have to use in your application. Most of the time, you can use one animated value and just interpolate on it, even in complex animations.

The Animated API interpolate function is quite powerful. You can have multiple values to define the range, extrapolate or clamp beyond the ranges, or specify the easing function of the animation.

Getting to know the advanced options of the Animated API

The Animated API brings a lot of different options, which give you the possibility to create almost every animation you can imagine:

- You can do mathematical operations on animated values such as `add()`, `subtract()`, `divide()`, `multiply()`, `modulo()`, and more.

- You can combine animations sequentially using `Animated.sequence()`, or combine them at the same time using `Animated.parallel()` (you can even combine these options, too).

- You can also work with delayed animations with `Animated.delay()` or loop animations with `Animated.loop()`.

- There are also other options to change an `Animated.Value` component aside from `Animated.timing()`. One of them is to use `Animated.event()` to bind the scroll value of a `ScrollView` to an `AnimatedValue`.

The following example is very similar to the example in the *Understanding the architectural challenge of animations in React Native* section of this chapter. The code shows you how to use a scroll value as the driver of an animation:

```
const App = () => {
  const scrolling = useRef(new Animated.Value(0)).current;

  const interpolatedScale = scrolling.interpolate({
    inputRange: [-300, 0],
    outputRange: [3, 1],
    extrapolate: 'clamp',
  });
  const interpolatedTranslate = scrolling.interpolate({
    inputRange: [0, 300],
    outputRange: [0, -300],
    extrapolate: 'clamp',
  });

  return (
    <>
      <Animated.Image
        source={require('sometitleimage.jpg')}
        style={{
          ...styles.header,
```

```
                transform: [
                    {translateY: interpolatedTranslate},
                    {scaleY: interpolatedScale},
                    {scaleX: interpolatedScale}
                ]
            }}
        />
        <Animated.ScrollView
            onScroll={
                Animated.event([{nativeEvent: {contentOffset: {y:
                    scrolling,},},}],
                    { useNativeDriver: true },
                )
            }
        >
            <View style={styles.headerPlaceholder} />
            <View style={styles.content}>
            </View>
        </Animated.ScrollView>
        </>
    );
}
```

In this example, the native scroll event of the ScrollView is connected directly to the Animated.Value component. With the useNativeDriver: true property, the native driver is used; this means that the animation, which is driven by the scroll value, runs completely on the native thread.

The preceding example contains two interpolations of the scroll value: the first one scales the image when the ScrollView has been over-scrolled (which means the ScrollView returns negative scroll values), while the second one moves the image up while scrolling.

Again, due to the use of the native driver, all this interpolation is done on the native thread. This makes the Animated API very performant in this use case. You can read more about running animations based on user gestures in *Chapter 7, Handling Gestures in React Native*.

The Animated API also provides different easing methods alongside complex spring models. For more detailed information, please take a look at the official documentation at bit.ly/prn-animated-api.

As you can see, the Animated API is really powerful, and you can achieve nearly every animation goal with it. So, why are there even other solutions on the market when this very good animation library is built in? Well, the Animated API is far from perfect for every use case.

Understanding the pros and cons of the Animated API

The internal React Native Animated API is a very good solution for simple to mid-complexity animations. These are the most important pros of the Animated API:

- **Powerful API**: You can build nearly every animation.

- **No external library needed**: You don't have to add any dependencies to your project to use the Animated API. This means no additional maintenance effort or larger bundle size.

- **Smooth animations with the native driver**: When using the native driver, you can be sure that your animation runs at 60 fps.

There are also some cons of the Animated API, which you have to keep in mind when choosing the best animation solution for your project:

- **Complex animations become quite confusing**: Due to the structure of the Animated API, animations with lots of elements or very high complexity can get very confusing, and the code can become very hard to read and understand.

- **The native driver does not support all style properties**: When using the Animated API, you should definitely use the native driver. Since this driver does not support position or Flexbox properties, the Animated API is, essentially, limited to non-layout properties.

- **Animated.Value only supports numeric and string values**: It is not possible to work with objects or arrays as animation values. If the animation value is more complex, multiple `Animated.Value` components have to be used.

All in all, I would recommend the Animated API for small to medium complexity animations, when you don't already have other animation libraries in your project. However, let's look at another option: `react-native-animatable`.

Creating simple animations with react-native-animatable

There are a lot of animations that are reused in nearly every app. This is what `react-native-animatable` is all about. This library is built on top of the internal React Native Animated API and provides a very simple declarative and imperative API to use simple, predefined animations.

Starting with a simple example

The following code example describes a simple fade-in animation with `react-native-animatable` using the declarative method, along with a simple fade-out animation with `react-native-animatable` using the imperative method:

```
import React from "react";
import { View, Text, Pressable } from "react-native";
import * as Animatable from 'react-native-animatable';

const App = () => {
  const handleRef = ref => this.view = ref;
  const hideView = () => {
    this.view.fadeOutDown(2000);
  }
  return (
    <>
      <Animatable.View
        style={{
          backgroundColor: 'red'

        }}
        ref={handleRef}
        animation="fadeInUp"
        duration=2000
      />
      <Pressable onPress={hideView}>
        <Text>Hide View</Text>
      </Pressable>
    </>
  );
}
export default App;
```

In this example, `Animatable.View` is given one of the predefined `Animatable` animations as the animation property, and a duration that defines how long the animation runs. That is all you have to do to have an entrance animation.

As stated before, Animatable also supports imperative usage, which means that you can call Animatable functions on Animatable components. In this example, `this.view` contains a reference to `Animatable.View`, which makes it possible to call Animatable functions on it.

This is done when pressing the `Pressable`. Here, `hideView` is called, which then calls the predefined `fadeOutDown` Animatable function, which makes the view disappear over 2 seconds (2,000 ms).

Using the native driver

As we learned in the *Using the internal Animated API of React Native* section, using the native driver is crucial for achieving smooth animations. Since `react-native-animatable` is based on the Animated API, you should also configure your animations to use the native driver.

With `react-native-animatable`, this is done by adding `useNativeDriver={true}` as a property to the component you run the animation on.

> **Important note**
>
> Please check whether the predefined animation you want to use supports the native driver before using it with the native driver.

The `react-native-animatable` library is not limited to predefined animations. It also supports defining custom animations with a very simple API. Let's take a look at how this is done.

Working with custom animations

The following example shows you how to create a simple fade-in and move-up animation, just as we did in the previous section:

```
const fadeInUpCustom = {
  0: {
    opacity: 0,
    translateY: 50,
  },
  1: {
    opacity: 1,
    translateY: 0,
  },
};
```

The custom animations of `react-native-animatable` map the styles to the keyframes. In this example, we start with the first keyframe (0), and set the `opacity` value to 0 and the `translateY` value to 50. With the last keyframe (1), the `opacity` value should be 1 and the `translateY` value should be 0. Now this animation can be used as the animation property value of any Animatable component instead of the predefined string values.

Understanding the pros and cons of react-native-animatable

Built on the React Native Animated API, all pros and cons of the Animated API also apply to `react-native-animatable`. In addition to that, the following pros are worth mentioning:

- **Very easy to use**: `react-native-animatable` is by far the easiest library to create and use high-quality animations.
- **Declarative approach**: The declarative approach creates code that is easy to read and understand.

Since `react-native-animatable` is a library built on top of the Animated API, this additional layer also brings some cons:

- **Additional dependency**: You have to add `react-native-animatable` as an additional dependency to your project. This is especially important because, at the time of writing, the project wasn't maintained very actively. This means that if anything changes in the underlying Animated API, it can prevent you from upgrading your React Native project.
- **Limited API**: The predefined animations and the possibilities to create custom animations are limited. If you want to create complex animations, you should use another option.

Essentially, `react-native-animatable` is a simple library on top of the React Native Animated API. It simplifies working with animations and works best with simple, predefined animations. If you need these simple or standard animations and you are very limited in time to create your animations, `react-native-animatable` is the best option for you.

If you'd like to create more complex animations, please take a look at the following section.

Exploring Reanimated 2 – the most complete animation solution for React Native

Reanimated is by far the most complete and mature animation solution for React Native. It was an improved reimplementation of the React Native Animated API in the first place, but with version 2, the API changed and the library's capabilities increased greatly.

This section covers the following topics:

- Getting to know the Reanimated API with a simple example
- Understanding the architecture of Reanimated 2
- Understanding the pros and cons of Reanimated

Let's get started.

Getting to know the Reanimated API with a simple example

Essentially, the core concept of Reanimated 2 is as simple as the Animated API. There are animation values that can be changed, and these animation values power the animations.

The following code shows an animation that scales in a `View` component:

```
import React from "react";
import { Text, Pressable } from "react-native";
import Animated, { useSharedValue, useAnimatedStyle,
    Easing, withTiming } from 'react-native-reanimated';


const App = () => {
    const size = useSharedValue(0);

    const showView = () => {
      size.value = withTiming(100, {
        duration: 2000,
        easing: Easing.out(Easing.exp),
      });
    }

    const animatedStyles = useAnimatedStyle(() => {
      return {
        width: size.value,
        height: size.value,
        backgroundColor: 'red'
      };
    });
```

```
    return (
      <>
        <Animated.View style={animatedStyles} />
        <Pressable onPress={showView}>
          <Text>Show View</Text>
        </Pressable>
      </>
    );
}
```

When looking at this code, we realize three things:

- The structure is quite similar to the Animated API. There is a sharedValue, which is Animated.Value in Animated, and a withTiming function, which is the equivalent to Animated.timing in Animated. The style object for the Animated.View component is created using a useAnimatedStyle function and is then used as a style property.

- There is no useNativeDriver property.

- We are changing width and height values in the animation, so the layout properties get changed, which wasn't possible with the React Native internal Animated API.

One of the cool things about Reanimated is that you don't have to care about the native driver. Every animation with Reanimated is processed on the UI thread. Another cool thing is that every style property can be used.

If you compare this to the limitations of the Animated API, you immediately see how much more powerful Reanimated is.

To understand how this is done, let's take a look at the Reanimated architecture.

Understanding the architecture of Reanimated 2

Reanimated 2 is based on animation worklets. In this context, a **worklet** is a JavaScript function that runs on the UI thread. Reanimated 2 spawns a second, very minimalistic, JavaScript environment on the UI thread that handles these animation worklets.

This means it runs completely independently from the React Native JavaScript thread and the React Native bridge, which guarantees awesome performance even for complex animations. This worklet context uses the new React Native architecture.

Let's start with gaining an understanding of how to use worklets.

Starting to work with worklets

Let's take a look at the example from the *Understanding the architectural challenge of animations in React Native* section of this chapter. We have an animation that resizes or moves a title image based on the *Y* scroll value of a `ScrollView`. The following figure shows what's happening when implementing this example with Reanimated 2:

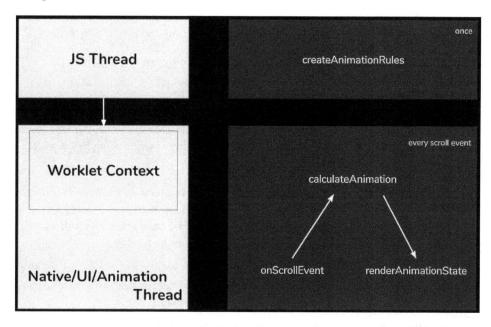

Figure 6.2 – Animation based on the scroll value in Reanimated 2

In Reanimated 2, the animation is created as a worklet on the JavaScript thread. But the whole animation worklet is executed in the worklet context on the UI thread. So, every time a new scroll event is received, it doesn't have to cross the bridge; instead, it's processed directly in the worklet context, and the new animation state is passed back to the UI thread for rendering.

To achieve this kind of architecture, Reanimated 2 comes with its own Babel plugin. This Babel plugin extracts every function that is annotated as `worklet` from the react-native code and makes it runnable in this separate worklet context on the UI thread. The following code example shows you how to annotate a function as a worklet:

```
function myWorklet() {
    'worklet';
    console.log("Hey I'm running on the UI thread");
}
```

This is a simple JavaScript function that contains the `worklet` annotation in line 2. Based on this annotation, the Reanimated 2 Babel plugin knows that it has to process this function.

Now, this can be run as a standard function on the JavaScript thread, but it can also be run as a worklet on the UI thread, depending on how it is called. If the function is called like a normal function in the JavaScript code, it runs on the JavaScript thread, and if it is called using the Reanimated 2 `runOnUI` function, it runs asynchronously on the UI thread.

Of course, it is possible to pass parameters to these worklet functions, no matter where it runs.

Understanding the connection between the JavaScript thread and the worklet context

Understanding this connection is crucial to prevent a lot of errors from happening. Essentially, the JavaScript thread and the worklet context run in completely different environments. This means it is not possible to simply access everything from the JavaScript thread while being in a worklet. The following connections are possible when it comes to worklets:

- **The JavaScript thread can start worklets and pass parameters**: As mentioned earlier, it is possible to run a function as a worklet when it has been annotated with `worklet` and is called with `runOnUI`. This runs the function in the worklet context on the UI thread. Every parameter that is passed is copied to the worklet context on the UI thread.

- **Worklets can access constants from the JavaScript thread**: Reanimated 2 processes the worklet code and copies the used constants and their values to the worklet context. This means constants can also be used in worklets without having to fear performance drops.

- **Worklets can invoke other worklet functions synchronously**: Worklets can call other worklets synchronously because they run in the same environment.

- **Worklets can call non-worklet functions asynchronously**: When functions on the JavaScript thread are called from within a worklet, this call has to be asynchronous because the invoked function runs in another environment.

For more information on worklets, you can take a look at the worklet part of the official documentation at `https://bit.ly/prn-reanimated-worklets`.

Using shared values

Like in the internal Animated API of React Native, Reanimated 2 works with animation values to drive the animation. These animation values are called **Shared Values** in Reanimated 2. They are called Shared Values because they can be accessed from both JavaScript environments – the JavaScript thread and the worklet context on the UI thread.

Since these Shared Values are used to drive animations, and these animations run in the worklet context on the UI thread, they are optimized to be updated and read from the worklet context. This means reads and writes of Shared Values from worklets are synchronous, while reads and writes from the JavaScript thread are asynchronous.

You can take a deeper look at Shared Values in the official documentation at `https://bit.ly/prn-reanimated-shared-values`.

Working with Reanimated 2 Hooks and functions

When working with Reanimated 2, there is no need to create worklets for most use cases. Reanimated 2 provides an excellent set of Hooks and functions that can be used to create, run, change, interrupt, and cancel animations. These Hooks take care of transferring the executions of the animation to the worklet context automatically.

This is what was used in the example at the beginning of this section. In that scenario, we created a Shared Value with the `useSharedValue` Hook, connected the View's style with the `useAnimatedStyle` Hook, and started the animation with the `withTiming` function.

Of course, you can also handle scroll values with Reanimated 2. The following code example shows you how to connect a `ScrollView` to a Shared Value, to scale and move an image with an animation driven by user scrolling:

```
function App() {
  const scrolling = useSharedValue(0);

  const scrollHandler = useAnimatedScrollHandler((event) =>
  {
    scrolling.value = event.contentOffset.y;
  });

  const imgStyle = useAnimatedStyle(() => {
    const interpolatedScale = interpolate(
      scrolling.value, [-300, 0], [3, 1], Extrapolate.CLAMP
    );
    const interpolatedTranslate = interpolate(
      scrolling.value, [0, 300], [0, -300], Extrapolate.CLAMP
    );
    return {
      transform: [
```

```
                    {translateY: interpolatedTranslate},
                    {scaleY: interpolatedScale},
                    {scaleX: interpolatedScale}
                ]
            };
        });


        return (
            <>
                <Animated.Image
                    source={require('sometitleimage.jpg')}
                    style={[styles.header, imgStyle]}
                />
                <Animated.ScrollView
                    onScroll={scrollHandler}          >
                    <View style={styles.headerPlaceholder} />
                    <View style={styles.content} />
                </Animated.ScrollView>
            </>
        );
    }
```

In this example, the ScrollView binds the Y scroll value (content offset) to the animation value using Reanimated's useAnimatedScrollHandler Hook. This animation value is then interpolated with the interpolate function of Reanimated 2. This is done inside a useAnimatedStyle hook.

This setup makes the animation work, without ever having to send scroll values over the bridge to the JavaScript thread. The whole animation runs inside the worklet context on the UI thread. This makes the animation extremely performant.

Of course, Reanimated 2 offers a wide range of other options. It is possible to use spring-based animations, velocity-based animations, delay or repeat animations, and run animations in sequence, just to name a few.

Since a complete guide on Reanimated 2 would go beyond the scope of this book, please have a look at the official documentation (https://bit.ly/prn-reanimated-docs) and the API reference (https://bit.ly/prn-reanimated-api-reference).

To complete this section, we will have a look at the pros and cons of Reanimated 2.

Understanding the pros and cons of Reanimated

Reanimated 2 is, by far, the most advanced and complete solution for animations in React Native. There are a lot of reasons to use Reanimated 2. Here is a list of the most important ones:

- **Easy-to-use API**: The Reanimated 2 API with Hooks and functions is easy to learn, read, and understand.

- **Awesome performance out of the box**: Animations with Reanimated 2 run smoothly and are performant on all devices out of the box.

- **Animation of layout properties**: All style values can be used in animations. There is no limitation like in the Animated API.

- **Interrupting, changing, and canceling animations**: Animations with Reanimated 2 can be interrupted, changed, or canceled while they run, without causing frame drops or sluggish behavior.

Reanimated 2 is a very good library, but before using it, you should have a look at the following cons:

- **Complicated installation**: Since Reanimated 2 deeply intervenes in the architecture of React Native, the installation is quite complicated. You have to make some changes to the native code and add the Reanimated 2 Babel plugin. This is not a big problem because it only has to be done once, but it will take some time. This will change when the new architecture, including the new Fabric renderer, is out.

- **Reanimated 2 makes you bundle larger**: While the internal Animated API is part of React Native, Reanimated 2 is an external dependency. This means your bundle will grow.

If you have an app with a lot of animations, more complex animations, and/or animated layout properties, I would definitely recommend using Reanimated 2. If you only use basic animations, which can be achieved with the internal Animated API, you don't need Reanimated and can stick to the Animated API.

While Reanimated 2, the Animated API, and even `react-native-animatable` have a very similar approach, the next library we will get to know works completely differently. Let's take a look at Lottie.

Using Lottie animations in React Native

Lottie is a completely different approach to animations in app and web development. It allows you to render and control prebuilt vector animations. The following figure shows the process of how a Lottie animation is created and played:

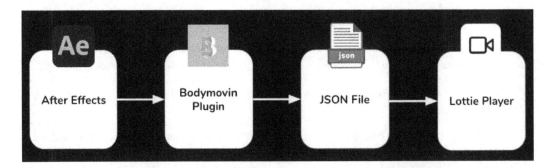

Figure 6.3 – The workflow when animating with Lottie

Essentially, Lottie consists of a player, which in the case of React Native is the `lottie-react-native` library. This library expects a JSON file of a Lottie animation. This file is created with Adobe After Effects (a professional animation software) and exported to JSON with the Bodymovin plugin.

This process completely changes the way we work with animations in apps. The developer is no longer responsible for creating the animations; they only have to include the JSON file. This can save a huge amount of time when working with very complex animations.

All of this becomes clearer when looking at a simple Lottie animation.

Starting with a simple example

The following code example shows the implementation of a loading animation with Lottie:

```
import React from 'react';
import { View, StyleSheet } from 'react-native';
import LottieView from 'lottie-react-native';

const App = () => {
    return (
        <View style={styles.center}>
            <LottieView
                source={require('loading-animation.json')}
                style={styles.animation}
                autoPlay/>
        </View>
    );
```

```
};

const styles = StyleSheet.create({
    center: {
        flex: 1,
            alignItems: 'center',
                justifyContent: 'center'
    },
    animation: {
        width: 150,
        height: 150
    }
});


export default App;
```

This is all the code that is needed to include a loading animation, no matter how complex the animation is. LottieView is imported from the `lottie-react-native` library and is placed where the animation should occur. The Lottie JSON file is passed as source to LottieView, which can be styled via the style property like a regular React Native view.

However, `lottie-react-native` is not just a simple player. It gives you programmatic control over the animation. You can start and stop the animation, autoplay it when it loads, and loop it so that it starts again after completion. The last one is especially useful for loading animations.

Combining Lottie animations with the React Native Animated API

The best feature of `lottie-react-native` is that it is possible to bind the progress of an animation to an `Animated.Value` component of the React Native Animated API. This opens up a lot of different use cases such as Lottie animations running time or spring-based. You can also use easing or create Lottie animations running based on user interaction.

The following code example shows you how to create a Lottie animation driven by an `Animated.Value` component that is bound to the Y scroll value of a React Native ScrollView:

```
const App = () => {
  const scrolling = useRef(new Animated.Value(0)).current;
  let interpolatedProgress = scrolling.interpolate({
    inputRange: [-1000, 0, 1000],
```

```
          outputRange: [1, 0, 1],
          extrapolate: 'clamp',
      });

      return (
        <View style={styles.container}>
          <Animated.ScrollView
            onScroll={Animated.event(
              [{
                nativeEvent: {
                  contentOffset: {
                    y: scrolling,
                  },
                },
              }],
              { useNativeDriver: true },
            )}
            scrollEventThrottle={16}>
              <LottieView
                source={require('looper.json')}
                style={styles.animation}
                progress={interpolatedProgress}/>
          </Animated.ScrollView>
        </View>
      )
  }
```

In this example, the *Y* scroll value of the ScrollView is bound to an Animated.Value component in the onScroll function of the ScrollView. Then, the Animated.Value component is interpolated to get an interpolatedProgress between 0 and 1. This interpolatedProgess is passed to LottieView as a progress property.

Lottie also supports animations of the React Native Animated API, that use the native driver. This is very important for performance reasons. For more on this, please read the *Using the internal Animated API of React Native* section of this chapter.

Finding or creating Lottie animations

While Lottie animations are very easy to include for the developer, someone has to create the Lottie JSON files that contain the animations. There are three ways to get Lottie animation files:

- **Find Lottie files on the internet**: There are a lot of talented animation artists out there who share their work on the internet. A lot of the files are free, but it is also possible to purchase premium animation content. The best place to start your search for Lottie animations is `https://lottiefiles.com/`.

- **Learn to create animations with After Effects**: There are a lot of good beginner tutorials, and even if it seems overwhelming to begin with, After Effects is an awesome software, and it is quite easy to create your first animations with it. If you are interested in learning After Effects, you can start with the tutorial at `bit.ly/prn-lottie-tutorial`.

- **Hire an animation artist**: This is, by far, the best solution from my point of view. An experienced animation artist will only need some hours to create a bunch of individual animations for your project. It will save you time and money to work with an animation artist, and it will greatly improve the quality of your app when having individual animations that exactly fit your UI concept. You can find and contact animation artists at `https://lottiefiles.com/`.

Now that we have a good understanding of how Lottie animations in React Native work, let's have a look at the pros and cons.

Understanding the pros and cons of Reanimated

Since the Lottie approach is completely different, there are huge pros and cons you should keep in mind when you consider using Lottie as the animation solution for your project.

The following pros stand out when using Lottie:

- **Lottie is the easiest solution for developers**: When working with `lottie-react-native`, it just takes a few lines of code to integrate an animation, no matter how complex it is.

- **Animations are much smaller than GIFs or Sprites**: Another approach when it comes to animated files is GIFs or Sprites. Lottie files are much smaller and consume far less memory than these solutions.

- **Programmatic control over the animation progress**: Unlike when working with GIFs, you have programmatic control over the animation. You can even bind the animation progress to the animation values of React Native Animated.

However, Lottie also comes with the following cons:

- **No full control over the animation**: When working with Lottie animations, you are able to control the progress of the animation, but only the progress. You cannot change the paths of the animations based on user interaction like you can when completely scripting the animation.

- **The large size of the Lottie library**: Lottie for React Native increases the bundle size. Depending on what platform an app is exported to, not only does `lottie-react-native` has to be included in the app but also the Lottie module for the native platform.

- **External dependency**: Lottie is an external dependency, and you have to keep in mind that this could slow down your update capabilities for new React Native versions. Since Lottie is not a React Native-only solution but also working on native apps and the web and React Native is a smaller platform compared to the other platforms Lottie is working on, it is kind of a second class citizen. This means it is not guaranteed that `lottie-react-native` will immediately work with every new React Native version.

Lottie is an awesome option to include high-quality animations in a React Native project. Especially for complex loading animations, micro-animations, or any animation where no complete programmatic control is needed, Lottie is a great solution.

Summary

In this chapter, you learned about the general architectural challenge when it comes to animations in React Native. You understood that there are different solutions to overcome this challenge and create high-quality and performant animations. With Animated, `react-native-animatable`, Reanimated, and Lottie, we looked at the best and the most widely used animation solutions for React Native's on-screen animations.

This is important because you will have to use animations in your app to create a high-quality product, and such animation libraries are the only way to create high-quality and performant animations in React Native.

In the next chapter, you will learn how to handle user gestures and also work with more complex user gestures to do different things – for example, to drive animations.

7

Handling Gestures in React Native

One of the most important things that makes good apps stand out against bad apps or mobile websites is good gesture handling. While mobile websites only listen to simple clicks in most cases, apps can and should be controlled with different gestures such as short touches, long touches, swipes, pinching to zoom, or touches with multiple fingers. Using these gestures in a very intuitive way is one of the most important things to consider when developing an app.

But it doesn't stop with just listening to these gestures – you have to give an immediate response to the user so that they can see (and maybe abort) what they are doing. Some gestures need to trigger or control animations and therefore have to play together very well with the animation solutions we learned about in *Chapter 6, Working with Animations*.

In React Native, there are multiple ways to handle gestures. From simple built-in components to very complex third-party gesture handling solutions, you have a lot of different options to choose from.

In this chapter, you will learn about the following:

- Using built-in components to respond to user gestures
- Working with the React Native gesture responder system and React Native `PanResponder`
- Understanding React Native Gesture Handler

Technical requirements

To be able to run the code in this chapter, you have to set up the following things:

- A working React Native environment (`bit.ly/prn-setup-rn` – React Native CLI Quickstart)
- A real iOS or Android device for testing gestures and multitouch

To access the code for this chapter, follow this link to the book's GitHub repository:

Using built-in components to respond to user gestures

React Native ships with multiple components that have built-in gesture responder support. Basically, these components are an abstracted use of the gesture responder system, which you will learn about in the next section. The gesture responder system provides support for handling gestures in React Native, as well as support for negotiating which component should handle the user gesture.

The simplest user interaction is a tap with one finger. With different `Touchable` components, a `Pressable` component, and a `Button` component, React Native provides different options for how to recognize the tap and respond to the user interaction.

Using components to respond to simple taps

The simplest components to record user taps are the React Native `Touchable` components.

Working with Touchable components

React Native provides three different `Touchable` components on iOS and an extra fourth `Touchable` component just for Android:

- `TouchableOpacity`: Provides user feedback automatically by reducing the opacity of the tapped element (and all child elements), letting the underlying view shine through. You can configure the opacity reduction by setting `activeOpacity`.

- `TouchableHighlight`: Provides user feedback automatically by reducing the opacity and showing an underlying color, which darkens or lightens the tapped element. You can define the underlying color by setting `underlayColor` and the opacity reduction by setting `activeOpacity`.

- `TouchableWithoutFeedback`: Provides no user feedback. You should only use this if you have a good reason since every element that responds to touches should show visual feedback. One reason could be that you handle the visual feedback somewhere else.

- `TouchableNativeFeedback`: For Android only. Provides user feedback automatically by triggering the native Android touch effect. On most devices, this is the well-known Android ripple effect, where the component changes the color by growing a circle from the point of touch. You can define the ripple effect by setting the `background` property.

All four `Touchable` components provide four methods to listen to user interaction. These methods are called in the order of the following figure:

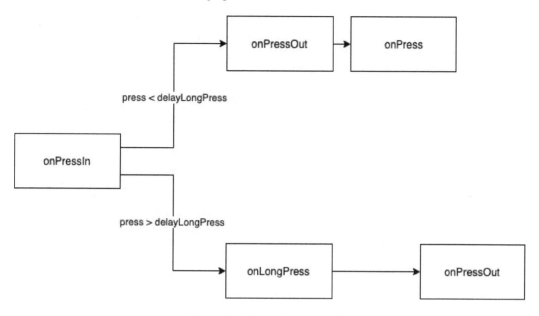

Figure 7.1 – The onPress call order

The important thing to always keep in mind is that `onPress` is called after `onPressOut`, while `onLongPress` is called before `onPressOut`. Let's have a look at the methods in more detail:

- `onPressIn`: The method is called immediately when the user starts tapping the button.
- `onPressOut`: The method is called when the user releases the tap or when the user moves the finger outside of the component.
- `onPress`: The method is called when the user completes the tap before a long press delay (defined in `delayLongPress`) is reached.
- `onLongPress`: The method is called when the long press delay (defined in `delayLongPress`) is reached and the tap wasn't released in the meantime.

With these methods, you can already handle a lot of different use cases and – never forget – give immediate visual feedback to user touches.

While the `Touchable` components need some own styling, React Native also provides a `Button` component, which comes with predefined styles.

Working with the Button component

Under the hood, `Button` uses `TouchableOpacity` on iOS and `TouchableNativeFeedback` on Android. `Button` comes with some predefined styling so that you can use it without styling it on your own. The following code example shows how simple it is to use `Button`:

```
<Button
  onPress={() => Alert.alert("Button pressed!")}
      title="Press me!"
      color="#f7941e"
/>
```

You only have to define an `onPress` method, a button `title`, and the `color` of the button. `Button` then handles the rest such as styling and visual user feedback. Of course, you can use all other methods of the `Touchable` components, too.

`Button` and `Touchable` are quite old components in React Native. Since they work well, you can use them in most cases. But there is also a new implementation for handling user taps.

Working with the Pressable component

Besides the `Touchable` and `Button` components, React Native also comes with a `Pressable` component. This is the latest component and is recommended to be used due to its advanced support for platform-specific visual feedback.

Have a look at the following code example to understand the advantages of `Pressable`:

```
<Pressable
  onPress={() => Alert.alert("Button pressed!")}
  style={({ pressed }) => [
    {
      backgroundColor: pressed
        ? '#f7941e'
        : '#ffffff'
    },
    styles.button
  ]}
>
  {
    ({ pressed }) => (
      <Text style={styles.buttonText}>
```

```
              {pressed ? 'Button pressed!' : 'Press  me!'}
        </Text>
      )
    }
  </Pressable>
```

It provides the same methods as the `Touchable` components, but it also has ripple support on Android and works with custom styling on iOS. You can provide the `style` property as a function and listen to the `pressed` state.

You can also pass a functional component as a child to the `Pressable` component and use the `pressed` state there. This means you can change the styling and content of the `Pressable` component based on whether it is pressed at the moment or not.

Another advantage is that you can define hit and offset areas for the `Pressable` component:

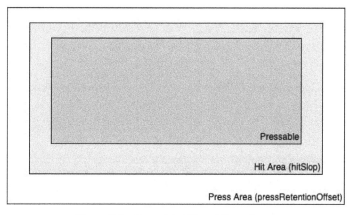

Figure 7.2 – Pressable Hit and Press Areas

In *Figure 7.2*, you can see the visible `Pressable` component in the center. If you want the touchable area to be larger than the visible element, you can do this by setting `hitSlop`. This is a very common thing to do for important buttons or important tappable areas of the screen.

While `hitSlop` defines the area where the tap starts, `pressRetentionOffset` defines the additional distance outside of the `Pressable` component where the tap does not stop. This means when you start a tap inside the Hit Area and move your finger outside of the Hit Area, normally `onPressOut` is fired and the tap gesture is completed.

But if you have defined an additional Press Area and your gesture stays inside this Press Area, the tap gesture is considered a lasting gesture as long as your finger moves outside this Press Area. `hitSlop` and `pressRetention` can either be set as a `number` value or as a `Rect` value, which means as an `Object` with `bottom`, `left`, `right`, and `top` properties.

Hit Area and Press Area are both great methods to improve the user experience of your app as, for example, they can make it easier for users to press important buttons.

After looking at simple tap handling, let's continue with scroll gestures.

Working with ScrollView

The simplest method to handle scroll gestures is React Native `ScrollView`. This component makes the content inside of it scrollable if the content is larger than `ScrollView` itself. `ScrollView` detects and handles scroll gestures automatically. It has a lot of options you can configure, so let's have a look at the most important ones:

- `horizontal`: Defines whether `ScrollView` should be horizontal or vertical. The default is vertical.

- `decelerationRate`: Defines how fast the scrolling will decelerate when the user releases the touch while scrolling.

- `snapToInterval` or `snapToOffsets`: With these two methods, you can define intervals or offsets at which `ScrollView` should stop. This can improve the user experience a lot because the scroll view can, for example, always stop so that the user can see a complete list element.

- `scrollEventThrottle` for iOS only: Defines how often a scroll event will be triggered while scrolling. This is very important for performance and UX reasons. The best value for UX is 16, which means the scroll event is fired every 16 ms (until RN supports 120 Hz – then, it will become 8 ms).

  Based on what you are doing with the scroll event, this can lead to performance problems because the scroll event is sent over the bridge every single time (unless you process it directly via the Animated API, as described in *Chapter 6, Working with Animations*). So, think about what value you need here and perhaps increase it to prevent performance problems.

> **Tip**
> There are a lot more configuration options such as defining over-scroll effects, sticky headers, or bounces. If you want to have a complete overview, please have a look at the documentation (`https://bit.ly/prn-scrollview`). Since this is not a beginner's guide, we are focusing on the parts that are important to optimize your application.

Speaking of which, you can of course handle the scroll events by yourself when using the `ScrollView` component. This gives you a variety of options on how to optimize your UX. `ScrollView` provides the following methods:

- `onScroll`: Fires continuously during scrolling. This is a great tool to add awesome user feedback to the scroll gesture by coupling custom animations to the scroll event, as we did in *Chapter 6, Working with Animations*. But when doing so, you should either work with the

Animated API with the native driver to prevent the scroll events from being transferred over the bridge every 16 ms or use `scrollEventThrottle` to limit the event count.

- `onScrollBeginDrag`: Fires when the user starts the scrolling gesture.

- `onScrollEndDrag`: Fires when the user stops the scrolling gesture.

- `onMomentumScrollBegin`: Fires when `ScrollView` starts moving.

- `onMomentumScrollEnd`: Fires when `ScrollView` stops moving.

With these five methods, you can give your users a lot of different feedback for a scroll gesture. From simply informing the user when they are scrolling to building advanced animations with `onScroll`, everything is possible.

> **Notice**
>
> `ScrollView` can become quite slow and memory hungry when it has a very long list of elements as children. This is due to `ScrollView` rendering all children at once. If you need a more performant version with lazy loading of elements, please have a look at React Native `FlatList` or `SectionList`.

After working with the built-in React Native components, it's time to have a look at handling touches completely by yourself. The first option to do that is to work directly with the React Native gesture responder system.

Working with the gesture responder system and PanResponder

The gesture responder system is the foundation of handling gestures in React Native. All the `Touchable` components are based on the gesture responder system. With this system, you can not only listen to gestures but you can also specify which component should be the touch responder.

This is very important because there are several scenarios in which you have multiple touch responders on your screen (for example, `Slider` in a `ScrollView`). While most of the built-in components negotiate which component should become a touch responder and should handle the user input on their own, you have to think about it yourself when working directly with the gesture responder system.

The gesture responder system provides a simple API and can be used on any component. The first thing you have to do when working with the gesture responder system is to negotiate which component should become the responder to handle the gesture.

Becoming a responder

To become a responder, a component must implement one of these negotiation methods:

- `onStartShouldSetResponder`: If this method returns `true`, the component wants to become the responder at the start of a touch event.

- `onMoveShouldSetResponder`: If this method returns `true`, the component wants to become the responder of a touch event. This method is called for every touch move event, as long as the component is not the responder.

> **Important tip**
>
> These two methods are called on the deepest node first. This means that the deepest component will become the responder to the touch event when multiple components implement these methods and return `true`. Please keep that in mind when manually negotiating the responders.
>
> You can prevent a child component from becoming the responder by implementing `onStartShouldSetResponderCapture` or `onMoveShouldSetResponderCapture`.

For these responder negotiations, it is important for a component to release control if another component asks for it. The gesture responder system also provides handlers for this:

- `onResponderTerminationRequest`: If this handler returns `true`, the component releases the responder when another component wants to become the responder.

- `onResponseTerminate`: This handler is called when the responder was released. This can be due to `onResponderTerminationRequest` returning `true` or due to OS behavior.

When a component tries to become the responder, there are two possible outcomes from the negotiation, which can both be handled with a handler method:

- `onResponderGrant`: This handler is called when it successfully became the responder and will then listen to touch events. It is best practice to use this method to highlight the component so that the user can see the element that responds to their touches.

- `onResponderReject`: This handler is called when another component is currently the responder and will not release control.

When your component successfully becomes the responder, you can use handlers to listen to the touch events.

Handling touches

After becoming the responder, there are two handlers you can use to capture the touch events:

- onResponderMove: This handler is called when the user moves their finger on the screen.

- onResponderRelease: This handler is called when the user releases their touch from the device's screen.

When working with gestures, you normally use onResponderMove and process the position values of the event it returns. When concatenating the positions, you can recreate the path the user draws on the screen. You can then respond to this path in the way you want.

How this works in practice is shown in the following example:

```
const CIRCLE_SIZE = 50;
export default (props) => {
  const dimensions = useWindowDimensions();
  const touch = useRef(
    new Animated.ValueXY({
      x: dimensions.width / 2 - CIRCLE_SIZE / 2,
      y: dimensions.height / 2 - CIRCLE_SIZE / 2
    })).current;
  return (
    <View style={{ flex: 1 }}
      onStartShouldSetResponder={() => true}
      onResponderMove={(event) => {
        touch.setValue({
          x: event.nativeEvent.pageX, y: event.nativeEvent.pageY
        });
      }}
      onResponderRelease={() => {
        Animated.spring(touch, {
          toValue: {
            x: dimensions.width / 2 - CIRCLE_SIZE / 2,
            y: dimensions.height / 2 - CIRCLE_SIZE / 2
          },
```

```
                    useNativeDriver: false
            }).start();
        }}
    >
        <Animated.View
            style={{
                position: 'absolute', backgroundColor: 'blue',
                    left: touch.x, top: touch.y,
                    height: CIRCLE_SIZE, width: CIRCLE_SIZE,
                    borderRadius: CIRCLE_SIZE / 2,
            }}
            onStartShouldSetResponder={() => false}
        />
    </View>
    );
};
```

This example contains two `View`. The outer `View` serves as the touch responder, while the inner `View` is a small circle, which changes position based on where the user moves the finger. The outer `View` implements the gesture responder system handlers, while the inner `View` just returns `false` for `onStartShouldSetResponder`, to not become the responder.

You also can see how the gesture responder system works with React Native Animated. When `onResponerMove` is called, we process the touch event and set the `pageX` and `pageY` values of the event to an `Animated.ValueXY`.

This is the value we then use to calculate the position of the inner `View`. When the user removes the finger from the device, `onResponderRelease` is called and we use an `Animated.spring` function to revert the `Animated.ValueXY` value back to its starting value. This positions the inner `View` back in the middle of the screen.

The following image shows how the code from the example looks on the screen:

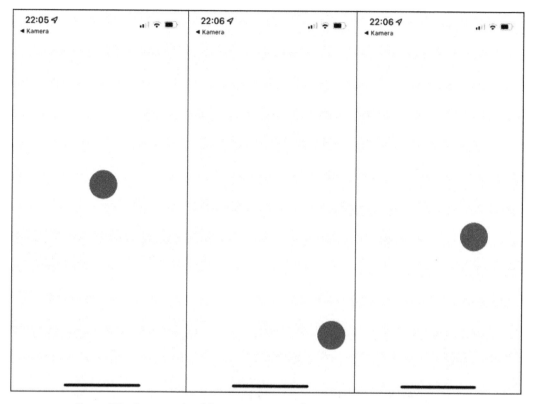

Figure 7.3 – An example of the gesture responder system running on an iPhone

Here, you can see the starting state (the left-hand screen). Then, the user touches the bottom right of the screen and the blue circle follows the touch (mid-screen). After the user releases the touch, the blue circle returns to the center of the screen from the position where the user last touched the screen over a given time period (the right-hand screen shows the circle during the return animation).

Even with this simple example, you can see that the gesture responder system is a very powerful tool. You have full control over the touch events and can combine them with animations very easily. Nevertheless, most of the time, you won't use the gesture responder system directly. This is because of PanResponder, which is a lightweight layer on top of the gesture responder system.

Using PanResponder

`PanResponder` basically works exactly as the gesture responder system does. It provides a similar API; however, you just have to replace `Responder` with `PanResponder`. For example, `onResponderMove` becomes `onPanResponderMove`. The difference is that you don't just get the raw touch events. `PanResponder` also provides a state object, which represents the state of the whole gesture. This includes the following properties:

- `stateID`: A unique identifier of the gesture
- `dx`: The horizontal distance since the start of the touch gesture
- `dy`: The vertical distance since the start of the touch gesture
- `vx`: The current horizontal velocity of the touch gesture
- `vy`: The current vertical velocity of the touch gesture

This state object can be very useful when it comes to interpreting and processing more complex gestures. Due to this, most libraries and projects use `PanResponder` instead of working directly with the gesture responder system.

While the gesture responder system and `PanResponder` are very good options to respond to user touches, they also come with some downsides. First of all, they have the same limitations as the Animated API without the native driver. Since the touch events have to be transferred via the bridge to the JavaScript thread, we always are one frame behind.

This may become better with the JSI, but this has to be proven at this point. Another limitation is that no API allows us to define any interaction between the native gesture handlers. This means there will always be cases, which are not solvable with the gesture responder system API.

Because of these limitations, the team at Software Mansion with the support of Shopify and Expo built a new solution – React Native Gesture Handler.

Understanding React Native Gesture Handler

React Native Gesture Handler is a third-party library that completely replaces the built-in gesture responder system while offering more control and higher performance.

React Native Gesture Handler works best in combination with Reanimated 2 because it was written by the same team and relies on the worklets provided by Reanimated 2.

> **Information**
> This book refers to React Native Gesture Handler version 2.0. Version 1 is also used in a lot of projects.

The React Native Gesture Handler 2 API is based on `GestureDetectors` and `Gestures`. While it does also support the API from version 1, I would recommend using the new API, as it is easier to read and understand.

Let's create the draggable circle example from the previous section, but this time we use React Native Gesture Handler and Reanimated 2:

```
const CIRCLE_SIZE = 50;
export default props => {
  const dimensions = useWindowDimensions();
  const touchX = useSharedValue(dimensions.width/
      2-CIRCLE_SIZE/2);
  const touchY = useSharedValue(dimensions.height/
      2-CIRCLE_SIZE/2);
  const animatedStyles = useAnimatedStyle(() => {
    return {
      left: touchX.value, top: touchY.value,
    };
  });
  const gesture = Gesture.Pan()
   .onUpdate(e => {
    touchX.value = e.translationX+dimensions.width/
        2-CIRCLE_SIZE/2;
    touchY.value = e.translationY+dimensions.height/
        2-CIRCLE_SIZE/2;
  })
   .onEnd(() => {
    touchX.value = withSpring(dimensions.width/
        2-CIRCLE_SIZE/2);
    touchY.value = withSpring(dimensions.height/
        2-CIRCLE_SIZE/2);
  });
  return (
    <GestureDetector gesture={gesture}>
      <Animated.View
        style={[
          {
            position: 'absolute', backgroundColor: 'blue',
              width: CIRCLE_SIZE, height: CIRCLE_SIZE,
```

```
            borderRadius: CIRCLE_SIZE / 2
        },
        animatedStyles,
      ]}
    />
  </GestureDetector>
);
};
```

In this example, you can see how React Native Gesture Handler works. We create `GestureDetector` and wrap it with the element representing the target of the touch gesture. Then, we create a `Gesture` and assign it to `GestureDetector`. In this example, this is a `Pan` gesture, which means it recognizes dragging on the screen. `Gesture.Pan` provides a lot of different handlers. In this example, we use two:

- `onUpdate`: This handler is called every time any position of the gesture updates
- `onEnd`: This handler is called when the gesture is released

We use `onUpdate` to change the value of our Reanimated `sharedValue` and `onEnd` to reset the `sharedValue` to the initial state.

We then use the `sharedValue` to create `animatedStyle`, which we assign to our `Animated.View`, which is our circle.

The outcome on the screen is the same as in the previous section, but we have two important advantages here:

- **Better performance**: Since we use Reanimated 2 worklets, our values and our calculation don't have to pass the bridge. The gesture input and the animation are completely calculated on the UI thread.
- **More options**: When we want to have more complex gesture handling, React Native Gesture Handler gives us a lot more opportunities compared to the built-in gesture responder system. For example, we can define relations between gestures and decide whether only one gesture can become active at a time (`Race`) or whether multiple gestures can become active at a time (`Simultaneous`).

In addition to that, React Native Gesture Handler ships with a lot of different gestures, such as `Tap`, `Rotation`, `Pinch`, `Fling`, or `ForceTouch`, as well as built-in components such as `Button`, `Swipeable`, `Touchable`, or `DrawerLayout`, which makes it a very good replacement for the built-in gesture responder system.

If you want to get a deeper understanding of all the possible options you have with React Native Gesture Handler, please have a look at the documentation: `bit.ly/prn-gesture-handler`.

Summary

In this chapter, we learned about React Native's built-in components and solutions to handle user gestures. From simple gestures such as single taps to more complex gestures, React Native provides stable solutions to handle gestures. We also had a look at React Native Gesture Handler, which is a great third-party replacement for these built-in solutions.

I would recommend using React Native's built-in components and solutions for all use cases where you can stick to the standard components. As soon as you start writing your own gesture handling, I would recommend using React Native Gesture Handler.

After Animations and Gesture Handling, we will proceed with another topic, which is very important in terms of performance.

In the next chapter, you will learn what different JavaScript engines are, what options you have in React Native, and what impact the different engines have on performance and other important key metrics.

JavaScript Engines and Hermes

React Native runs on JavaScript and, as mentioned in *Chapter 2, Understanding the Essentials of JavaScript and TypeScript*, JavaScript needs a JavaScript engine to interpret and/or transform the code into executable machine code. There is no exception to this for React Native.

While there are quite a lot of different JS engines out there, only a few are used in React Native projects. This is due to the quite complex process to change the JS engine as well as the new Hermes engine, which is an engine developed for React Native and is going to be the default soon. Nevertheless, it is important and helpful to understand the different possible engines with their strengths and weaknesses.

In this theoretical chapter, we will cover the following topics:

- Understanding JavaScript engines
- Getting to know the Hermes engine
- Comparing key metrics

Technical requirements

Since this is a theoretical chapter, you don't need to have anything set up.

Understanding JavaScript engines

As mentioned in the introduction to this chapter, a JavaScript engine is responsible for interpreting JavaScript and/or transforming it into machine code, so that the device can execute it.

The first JavaScript engines were simple interpreters that simply processed the statements and ensured the execution. The code was just executed like it was written. This has changed a lot.

Modern JS engines provide a lot of optimization features. The most discussed is **just-in-time** (**JIT**) compilation, which is implemented by all modern JS engines.

Compiled languages such as C are compiled before the execution of the code. In this compile step, the transformation to machine language is done as well as a lot of optimization steps. This creates an output that is extremely performant.

Just-in-time compilation means that the code is compiled while it runs. This means the just-in-time compiler does not know all the code while it compiles. This makes code optimization a lot more difficult. The just-in-time compiler contains two components – the **profiler** and the **compiler**. While the JS code is executed by the interpreter, the profiler keeps an eye on how often the different statements are executed.

The more often a statement is executed, the higher priority it gets from the profiler. When a certain threshold is hit, the profiler sends these statements of code to the compiler, which then compiles the statements to bytecode. When the statement shall be executed the next time, it is done via a highly optimized bytecode interpreter. This makes these sections run much faster.

There are some more optimizations that can be done during the compilation. This depends a lot on the implementation and every modern JS engine has its own just-in-time compiler implementation.

In general, just-in-time compilation works better for longer running code, because then the compiler has more time to learn how to optimize. Since a lot of JS code is executed while running a React Native app, just-in-time compilation works great.

The most widely known JS engines today are JavaScriptCore and V8. Since both can be used in React Native, we'll have a deeper look at them.

Using JavaScriptCore

JavaScriptCore is the JS engine that powers the Safari browser. It is the default engine shipping with React Native. If you create a new blank project, JavaScriptCore will interpret and execute your JS code.

Using V8

V8 is an open source JS engine, heavily backed by Google. It is used by default when you are using the remote debugging feature of React Native. In this case, your JS code is executed in your Chrome browser, which is powered by V8.

> **Important tip**
> Please always keep in mind that you are using different JS engines when having remote debugging on/off. Without remote debugging, your JS code runs on your device or simulator; with remote debugging activated, your JS code runs on your computer in Chrome and communicates with native via WebSockets. Even if the two engines should behave quite similarly, there are some inconsistencies. So always test without remote debugging before shipping your app.

There is also a project that provides support for V8 as the main JS engine for React Native. This is no big deal for Android since it just replaces the JavaScriptCore for Android JS engine with the V8 engine. It gets more complex on iOS since JavaScriptCore is available on iOS without having to include it in the app bundle. So instead of just using the available JS engine, you would have to bundle the V8 engine in your app. This increases your app bundle size by up to 7 MB depending on the version you use. You can find more information on this on the `react-native-v8` project: `https://bit.ly/prn-rn-v8`.

While both engines work fine, Facebook started a project called **Hermes** to develop their own JS engine for React Native. The use case of React Native differs a lot from that of the browser engines as the code is available at build time and cannot change after shipping; hence, there is a lot more room for optimization.

Getting to know the Hermes engine

Hermes was brought to the React Native community at the React Native EU conference in 2019. Back then, it was already in production in Facebook's apps for more than a year. It is completely built with mobile in mind, which changes the architectural approach completely. The following figure shows how a modern JS engine works.

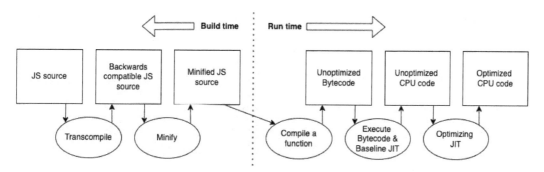

Figure 8.1 – Modern JS engine pipeline (inspired by Tsvetan Mikov)

When creating and building JavaScript code, usually there is some transcompiling done to backward-compatible JS code and some JS code minification. This minified JS bundle is then sent to a device and gets executed. JS engines such as JavaScriptCore or V8 try to optimize the execution using just-in-time compilation, which, as described before, is a quite complex process and may store and optimize the wrong code statements. Hermes changes the way this is done completely.

The following figure shows how optimization and compilation are done in Hermes:

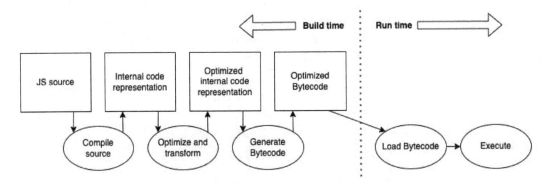

Figure 8.2 – Hermes pipeline (inspired by Tzvetan Mikov)

Because we know all the code, we want to ship in our React Native app, it is possible to do the compilation and optimization during the build process. This means all optimization is done on your computer (or in your CI environment) and not on the users' devices. Hermes uses a so-called internal code representation, which is highly optimized for the optimization of code.

After optimizing the code, it is compiled to optimized bytecode. So, when working with Hermes, you don't ship JavaScript any longer, you ship optimized bytecode. This bytecode only has to be loaded and executed by the Hermes engine on the users' devices.

This approach brings a lot of benefits. The most important are as follows:

- **No warmup**: We don't need to spend time on just-in-time compiler warmup.
- **No memory usage for just-in-time compiler output**: We don't need any memory for the output of the just-in-time compiler. This reduces the memory footprint a lot.
- **Startup optimizations**: Some operations that are done by JS engines at startup can be precomputed. This makes the start of the application a lot faster.
- **Smaller bundle size**: The optimized bundle is smaller than minified JavaScript code.

Due to the benefits of this approach, Hermes is pushed to become the default JS engine for React Native as soon as possible. At the point of writing, you still have to activate it, but it is quite simple:

- **Android**: Go to your `android/app/build.gradle` file and change `enableHermes` from `false` to `true`. You have to clean and rebuild your application after that.
- **iOS**: Go to your `ios/Podfile` file and change `:hermes_enabled => false` to `:hermes_enabled => true`. Reinstall your pods with `cd ios && pod install`.

Please note that the remote debugging feature does work differently when using Hermes. Since the approach is completely different, there is no bundle that can be run directly in your Chrome browser. Nevertheless, Hermes does support debugging with the Chrome inspector protocol and the Chrome developer tools.

To use remote debugging, you have to connect your Chrome browser to your running device via Metro. This is done as follows:

1. Go to `chrome://inspect/#devices` in your Chrome browser.
2. Click on the `Configure...` button and add the Metro server address (usually `localhost:8081`).
3. Now, there is a `Hermes React Native` target, which you can inspect.

For more information, please visit the Hermes documentation of React Native (`https://bit.ly/prn-hermes`) or the documentation of the Hermes engine itself (`https://bit.ly/prn-hermes-engine`).

As mentioned, the Hermes approach brings a lot of benefits to React Native. This is also reflected in key metrics, which we are going to have a look at in the following section.

Comparing key metrics

When it comes to mobile apps, there are a few metrics you should have a look at when optimizing your application.

Understanding important metrics

The most important key metrics on mobile are the following:

*   **Time to interaction** (TTI): This is the time between the user clicking on your app icon and when the user can use your app. It is important to reduce the TTI as much as possible because mobile app users are very impatient. The longer the TTI is, the more users will leave your app without even using it.

*   **Application size**: This is the size the user has to download from the store to install your application. The larger the application size is, the more users won't download your app. This can have many reasons such as high transfer costs in some countries or disk space left on the user's device. The fact is, the smaller your app is, the more users will download it.

*   **Memory utilization**: This metric describes how much memory your application consumes during execution. If your app is very memory-hungry, it can lead to problems, especially on older devices or during multitasking. Also, it can lead to the operating system closing your app. The less memory your app consumes, the better it is.

There are some benchmark results publicly available when looking at these metrics. As JavaScriptCore and V8 deliver mostly similar results (V8 is a bit better in most tests), we'll focus on the comparison of JavaScriptCore and Hermes used in a React Native application.

Comparing JavaScriptCore and Hermes on Android

The following test compares the key metrics of JSC and Hermes on Android. The test was run by the Hermes team at Facebook with a very early version of Hermes:

	JSC	Hermes		
Time to interaction	4.30s	2.01s	-2.29s	-53%
Application size	41MB	22MB	-19MB	-46%
Memory Utilization	185MB	136MB	-49MB	-26%

Figure 8.3 – Facebook JSC/Hermes test on Android (https://bit.ly/prn-hermes-test-fb)

There was another test run by Kudo Chien, a well-respected member of the React Native community, that also included TTI. This test also worked with different bundle sizes:

	JSC	Hermes	*in ms	
TTI 3MB bundle	400	240	160	-40%
TTI 10MB bundle	584	305	279	-48%
TTI 15MB bundle	694	342	352	-51%

Figure 8.4 – TTI test by Kudo Chien on Android (https://bit.ly/prn-hermes-test-kudo)

If you have a look at the test results, they are just remarkable on Android. The time to interaction was reduced by around 50% in all tests. This is a real game-changer. React Native apps used to open quite slowly compared to real native or Flutter apps. This is due to the need of initializing the JS engine before rendering their first screen. Hermes is a huge step in the right direction for React Native in this area.

When having a look at the Facebook test, the application size was also reduced by nearly 50%. This is partly because we don't have to bundle the JavaScriptCore engine into our application anymore, so this effect will reduce on larger applications. But you can expect a saving in bundle size by around 30% even on larger apps.

Now let's have a look at memory utilization. In Facebook's test, Hermes achieved memory savings of around 25%. This is mostly because of the not needed just-in-time compilation and is also a huge achievement.

Again, these tests were run with very early versions of Hermes, so you can expect larger gains in the future.

While the results are very clear on Android, let's proceed with tests on iOS.

Comparing JSC and Hermes on iOS

On iOS, we have to keep in mind that JavaScriptCore is provided by the operating system. This means when using JSC, we don't have to bundle any JavaScript engine into our application. Also, JavaScriptCore is optimized for iOS and Apple products. The implementation of Hermes on iOS was done by **Callstack**, a company that contributes a lot to React Native in general. After completing the implementation, the Callstack team also ran some tests to compare JSC and Hermes. These are the results:

	JSC	Hermes	*in ms	
Time to interaction	920ms	570ms	-350ms	-38%
Application size	10.6MB	13MB	2,4MB	18%
Memory utilization	216MB	178MB	-38MB	-18%

Figure 8.5 – Callstack JSC/Hermes test on iOS (https://bit.ly/prn-hermes-test-ios)

As on Android, time to interaction and memory utilization improved a lot. The values are a little lower than on Android, but this can be explained due to the better optimization of JSC on iOS. The application size increased on iOS, which seems only logical, so we now have to add Hermes to our bundle, while JSC is provided by the operating system.

But when the JavaScript bundle of your app grows, this effect will decrease due to the smaller bytecode of Hermes compared to the minified JS code shipped with the JSC-based bundle.

Summary

In this chapter, we had a look at JavaScript engines in general, learned about the special requirements React Native has for a JavaScript engine, the different engines we can use in React Native, and how to change the JS engine of our React Native project. We then had a look at Hermes, a JavaScript engine developed with mobile in general and React Native especially in mind.

After understanding the approach of Hermes and its benefits, we compared mobile app key metrics on apps running on JavaScriptCore, V8, and Hermes. While there is no big difference in using JSC or V8, Hermes brings a huge boost in terms of TTI and memory utilization to React Native.

After mastering JavaScript engines, we'll have a look at useful tools when working with React Native in the next chapter.

9

Essential Tools for Improving React Native Development

React Native is a framework with a very strong developer community. During the last year, there was an evolutionary growth of a large variety of tools and libraries, making the development of React Native apps a lot easier and a lot more comfortable.

Besides the tools and libraries developed especially for React Native, you can also use a lot of things in the plain React ecosystem. This is because most of these things are compatible with the JavaScript/React part of any React Native app.

Being aware of the best tools and libraries and how to use them is really useful because it saves you a lot of time and can greatly improve the quality of your code and product.

Especially when you are working on bigger projects, some tools are an absolute must-have to ensure good collaboration in a bigger team.

In this chapter, you will learn about the following topics:

- How to improve code quality with type safety, linters, and code formatters
- Why and when you should use boilerplate solutions and how to leverage them
- How to find and use high-quality UI libraries
- Why and when you should use Storybook and how to use it

Technical requirements

To be able to run the code in this chapter, you have to set up the following things:

- A working React Native environment (`https://reactnative.dev/docs/environment-setup`) – React Native CLI Quickstart

Improving code quality with type safety, linters, and code formatters

As already mentioned in *Chapter 2, Understanding the Essentials of JavaScript and TypeScript*, it is necessary to use typed JavaScript alongside some tools to ensure a certain level of quality in bigger projects.

In the following section, you will learn how to do this. Let's start with type safety using TypeScript or Flow.

Ensuring type safety with TypeScript or Flow

Type safety is standard in most programming languages such as Java or C#, and this is for good reason. In contrast, JavaScript is dynamically typed. This is because of the history of JavaScript. Remember, JavaScript was created as a scripting language to write small chunks of code very quickly. For this scenario, dynamic typing is fine, but when a project grows, static typing with all its advantages is a must-have.

Using typed JavaScript creates some overhead for creating your types at the beginning, but it gives you a lot of advantages at the end. Also, today, most libraries come with defined types, which you can use out of the box.

In *Chapter 2, Understanding the Essentials of JavaScript and TypeScript*, you already learned how to use and write TypeScript. This subsection focuses on the advantages of TypeScript and what errors you can prevent when using it.

Dynamic typing can lead to serious and hard-to-find errors

Let's start this section with a real-world example, which I experienced in one of my projects. While working on a React Native project, we used JavaScript without static typing. We fetched questions with a unique ID from a remote database (Google Firebase) and stored them locally on the device (AsyncStorage).

Based on the ID of the questions, we also stored user answers and marked the questions as answered in the app. After an update, all the answers seemed to be gone from the users' devices, and nobody understood why. It turned out that the update changed the unique IDs from number to string, which made the comparison between the stored user answers and the questions fail.

The debugging of this error was very hard because it didn't occur when answers were created with the updated version of the app. It only occurred when questions were answered in an older version of the app; following this, the app was then updated, and the questions were synced.

In addition to that, the error never threw an error message. It just happened silently. So, it took quite some time to find and fix the bug. This is just one example of an error that happens because of dynamic typing and why it is hard to deal with these errors. They can lead to hard errors, which you notice directly, but in a lot of cases, they don't.

This is especially severe in the case of app development, where you store a lot of data on the users' devices. When you don't realize that you have problems with your data types, this can lead to corrupt data on millions of different devices, which is really hard to recognize, debug, and fix.

Most of these errors can be prevented with static type checking using TypeScript or Flow.

> **Important note**
> When using TypeScript or Flow, don't use `any` or `Object` to make your life easier while writing your types. Type checking and all its advantages only really work when using it in the whole project. So, you should explicitly type all your properties.

Typed JavaScript doesn't only prevent bugs, it can also boost your productivity.

Enhancing your IDE with code completion

When you have statically defined types, it is easy for your IDE to help you with code completion. Most modern IDEs such as Visual Studio Code or JetBrains WebStorm have excellent support for TypeScript and Flow.

While WebStorm has most of the support built in for TypeScript and Flow, there are a lot of useful plugins for VS Code. Especially when working with Flow, you must install an extension for code completion and code navigation to work correctly. To do so, go to **Extensions** and search for `Flow Language Support`.

Additionally, I would recommend running type checks in every commit with your CI pipeline. You can read more about this in *Chapter 11, Creating and Automating Workflows*.

While typed JavaScript prevents a lot of errors and boosts productivity, there are many more areas where you can prevent errors from happening. Most of them are covered by linters. In the next section, you learn what they are and how they work.

Getting rid of the most common bugs with linters

Linters are tools that watch your code and enforce certain rules. When it comes to JavaScript/TypeScript, ESLint is, by far, the most popular and mature linter on the market, so this subsection will focus on ESLint. It analyzes your code and finds problems by checking your code against a predefined ruleset.

These problems can be errors, non-efficient code, or even code styling errors. I would recommend using ESLint because it comes at no cost and can ensure a certain level of code quality.

If you use the React Native CLI to set up your project, you will find ESLint preinstalled with a working ruleset. If you want to add it to an existing project, you can install it with the following commands: either use `npm install --save-dev eslint` or `yarn add --dev eslint`. In the next step, you have to set up a configuration. This can be done automatically with the `npm init @ eslint/config` or `yarn create @eslint/config` commands.

Now you can use ESLint to check your code against your ruleset with `npx eslint file.js` or `yarn run eslint file.js`. ESLint even comes with a `--fix` option, which automatically tries to fix as many errors as possible.

You can also integrate ESLint in most modern IDEs, to highlight and automatically fix problems found by ESLint. I would recommend doing so.

Additionally, I would recommend running ESLint checks in every commit with your CI pipeline. You can read more about that in *Chapter 11, Creating and Automating Workflows*.

ESLint is an awesome tool to find common errors, and even though it also supports code styling rules, there is another tool that does a better job in this area.

Enforcing a common code style with prettier

Prettier is a code formatter that was created in 2016. Essentially, it automatically rewrites your code based on a set of rules. This ensures that it follows standards and enforces a common code style for the whole development team of a project.

To use prettier, you can simply install it as a development dependency with the following commands. Either use `npm install --save-dev prettier` or `yarn add --dev prettier`.

It can be a bit challenging to integrate prettier with linters such as ESLint. This is because – as you learned in the previous subsection – these linters also have rules to format code. When you use both and have specified conflicting rules, this won't work. Fortunately, prettier comes with premade configs for ESLint, which prevent exactly that. You can download them from the prettier home page.

After the installation is complete, you can run prettier from the command line. To check whether your code styling follows the prettier rules, you can use the `prettier` command, followed by the path of a file or folder you want to check. In practice, you often want to make prettier format your files for you. This can be achieved with `prettier --write` followed by a path of a file or folder.

> **Important tip**
> You can use a `.prettierignore` file to exclude files from getting rewritten by prettier. You should use this file to prevent rewriting of files that are not written by you, config files, or others.

Prettier brings a lot of value to your project, and you will not want to develop without it, especially when you are not working alone. The most important advantages of using prettier are listed as follows:

- **Easier code reviews**: When doing code reviews, most editors highlight the changes that have been made. By far, the most annoying thing in a code review is when a developer has another autoformatting setting, resulting in all the code being marked as changed for the review. While this makes total sense because all the code has been changed due to autoformatting, it makes the review process a lot harder. It takes more time and makes it more vulnerable to errors in the review. Prettier prevents this by enforcing a common code style.

- **Easier code readability**: When you add developers to your team, code readability is an important factor. The easier the code readability is, the less time a new developer will need to be a productive part of your team. Prettier guarantees a common code style, which makes the code easier to read and understand.

Prettier is available as a command-line tool and as an IDE extension/plugin for all common IDEs. To ensure that it is used, you should include it in the following parts of your project:

- **IDE**: All developers should add prettier to their IDE and configure their autoformatting shortcut to use prettier.

- **Before Commit**: A before commit hook should ensure that prettier does not throw any errors.

- **CI/CD**: When creating a pull request/merge request, prettier should be run to ensure that the manual review can be done in an efficient manner. You can read more about this in *Chapter 11*, *Creating and Automating Workflows*.

If you implement this process with prettier, you will save a lot of time in the long run.

So, you learned about the most important tools while working with React Native projects. Now you will get to know some tools to successfully start new React Native projects. There are different open source **boilerplate solutions** on the market, all with their own advantages. A boilerplate solution means either a template you can use to start with or a CLI tool to generate your start project.

Using boilerplate solutions

Boilerplate solutions make it easy to set up a project with a solid architecture. This can be very helpful, but you should be aware of the trade-offs that come with these boilerplate solutions. Additionally, you should know exactly what you want because there are completely different solutions out there.

First, a boilerplate solution in this context is everything that creates code for you to start without having to configure everything on your own. This can be anything, from a simple template that has built-in TypeScript support but nothing else to a complete CLI solution that brings you solutions for navigation, state management, fonts, animations, connection, and more such as the Ignite CLI by Infinite Red.

Because there is such a wide range of what a boilerplate solution consists of, it's hard to make general assumptions about them. Nevertheless, what can be said is that the more that is packed into the boilerplate solution, the bigger the risk that anything inside is broken. Therefore, in this section, you will learn about the most common ones, every single solution with advantages, trade-offs, and how to use them.

Using the React Native TypeScript template

React Native comes with an integrated template engine. When you are using the React Native CLI to set up your project, you can work with a `template` flag. This is how you can use the React Native TypeScript template:

```
npx react-native init App
    --template react-native-template-typescript
```

This template does not come with any solution for navigation, state management, or anything else. It is the plain React Native Starter template, but with support for TypeScript. I like it very much because it is very simple, has nearly no dependencies, and lets you decide on what you need, while it does all the TypeScript compiler configuration for you.

Advantages of this include the following:

- TypeScript support
- No unwanted dependencies
- Easy to maintain

Trade-offs include the following:

- None

While the React Native TypeScript template is a no-brainer to use when starting a new project, the following boilerplate solutions are not that easy to decide on. This is because they come with more libraries attached.

Using React Native Boilerplate by thecodingmachine

This boilerplate also uses the built-in React Native template engine to work. But compared to the React Native TypeScript template, it already makes decisions on many things for you. It comes with Redux, Redux Persist, and the redux toolkit for state management, Axios for API calls, React Navigation, and Flipper integration. Additionally, it creates a good directory structure for your project. You can create a project based on this template with the following call:

```
npx react-native init MyApp
    --template @thecodingmachine/react-native-boilerplate
```

Because this template comes with a lot of predefined libraries, you should take a look at whether it is actively maintained and has been updated recently. Otherwise, you could start with very old versions of all the libraries that would need a potentially time-consuming update very soon.

Advantages of this include the following:

- TypeScript support
- Good libraries
- Good project structure

Trade-offs of this include the following:

- It uses Redux for State Management, so you might have to stick to that
- At the time of writing, it was already three versions behind the most recent React Native release, so you will miss the most recent features and bug fixes

For more information on this boilerplate, please visit the official documentation at `https://thecodingmachine.github.io/react-native-boilerplate/`.

While these are good solutions, you should have a look to see whether they really fit your project. The next template comes with a slightly different configuration.

Using React Native Starter Kit by mcnamee

This boilerplate does not use any template engine or CLI. It is just a GitHub repository that you can download or clone and start with. Additionally, it comes with a useful structure and brings a lot of libraries.

It uses Redux and Rematch for state management, React Native Router Flux for navigation, and it also comes with Native Base as the UI library and Fastlane for deployment. Essentially, it brings you all you need to get your first result shipped in hours.

But again, please have a look at how well-maintained the template is. At the time of writing, the last release of React Native Router Flux was more than a year ago, which means one core library of the template is essentially unusable.

Advantages of this include the following:

- Good project structure
- Adds everything to get you going

Trade-offs of this include the following:

- It uses Redux for State Management, so you might have to stick to that

- It uses Native Base as UI Toolkit, so you might have to stick to that

- It has an outdated navigation library, so you will have problems with the most recent versions of React Native

You can find more information about this template from the official GitHub page at `https://github.com/mcnamee/react-native-starter-kit`.

After looking at two boilerplate templates, we'll have a look at two really extensive CLI tools to set up your project.

Working with Ignite CLI

Ignite is a boilerplate solution developed and maintained by Infinite Red, an awesome React Native company, doing awesome open source work. It is much more than a simple template. It is a complete CLI, replacing the built-in React Native `init` command.

With the following command, you can create a new app:

```
npx ignite-cli new YourAppName
```

This creates an application with a good folder structure, React Navigation for navigation, MobX-State-Tree for state management, apisauce for API calls, and, of course, TypeScript support. In addition to that, your project automatically supports Flipper and Reactotron for debugging, Detox for end-to-end tests, and Expo, including Expo web.

On top of all that, Ignite CLI comes with a feature called **generators**. With these generators, you can generate your models, components, screens, and navigators via the Ignite CLI. This means you can customize your project to your needs, without having to write these files from scratch. If you want to create a new component, you can use the following command:

```
npx ignite-cli generate component MyNewComponent
```

This command creates a component based on a template stored in the `ignite/templates` folder, which was created with your project.

> **Tip**
> When working with the Ignite generators, you can edit the templates that are used to generate your files. Just edit the templates in `ignite/templates`, and the generated files will include your changes. This means you can adapt the templates to your needs and standards, and then use the generators to ensure that everyone sticks to those standards.

While this setup is great for professional projects, it comes with a lot of library decisions built in. In particular, MobX-State-Tree for State Management is one you might want to have a look at. It is a great solution for state management, but it isn't as popular as Redux or React Context, which means the community support is quite poor.

Advantages of this include the following:

- Good project structure
- Good debugging integration
- Integration for Detox end-to-end testing
- Localization integration
- Generators

Trade-offs of this include the following:

- It uses MobX-State-Tree for State Management, which isn't as popular as Redux or React Context.
- It has Expo integration out of the box. This will grow your app bundle size and adds another dependency.
- It adds a lot of overhead for smaller projects

For more information on Ignite, please visit the GitHub page at `https://github.com/infinitered/ignite`.

Now you know different boilerplate solutions along with their advantages and trade-offs. Even if you don't use a boilerplate solution for creating your projects, I would recommend having a look at the structure they create. This kind of structure is something you can build on.

After looking at these boilerplate solutions, next, we'll focus on the UI part. There are also a lot of useful open source solutions out there, which will make your life a lot easier.

Finding and using high-quality UI libraries

UI libraries provide a predefined UI for the most common use cases. There are a lot of different UI libraries you can use for your project. But some are better than others. This section not only names the most popular ones, but it also gives you an idea of what you must look for when doing your own research.

A good UI library should meet the following criteria:

- **Well maintained**: As with all libraries, it has to be well maintained. This means there are multiple contributors, there is good code quality, and there are regular releases. This is important to ensure that future version upgrades of React Native are supported.

- **Component-based**: A React Native UI library should provide a set of components, which you can use out of the box.

- **Theming**: The library should include theming options and be easily adaptable to your colors, fonts, paddings, and margins.

- **Type declarations**: A good UI library should have type declarations for components and themes.

There are a lot of different UI libraries out there. I will introduce you to two of them in the following subsection, but since they don't have to be the best fit for your project, please do your own research based on the criteria mentioned here before using either of them.

Working with React Native Paper

React Native Paper is a UI library based on **Material Design**. It is created and maintained by Callstack, a React Native company that is also working a lot on the React Native core, so these folks know what they are doing. This means the library sets a very high standard regarding code quality.

React Native Paper meets all the criteria defined in the previous subsection. The following features are included in React Native Paper:

- **Excellent theming support**: Paper comes with integrated theming. You can easily change and extend the default themes and use them all over your app.

- **Type declarations**: All of the components and themes come with type declarations.

- **Icons**: Paper uses `react-native-vector-icons` and `MaterialCommunityIcons` to provide you with icons.

- **Over 30 pre-built components**: All components are highly customizable and easy to use.

- **Excellent React Navigation integration**: Paper integrates very well in the React Navigation library. This means you can use components such as `Appbar` as a custom navigation bar in React Navigation.

While React Native Paper is possibly the best UI library out there from a technical point of view, you must keep in mind that it is completely based on Google's Material Design. This means you might not want to use it on iOS, since it makes your app look different than the iOS standards.

For more information about React Native Paper, its installation, and its usage, please visit the official documentation at `https://callstack.github.io/react-native-paper/`.

Another high-quality UI library is NativeBase. In the next subsection, you will learn about this library.

Working with NativeBase

NativeBase is a UI library that works for React Native alongside plain React. This means it not only works within your iOS and Android app, but it also works on your web app if you have one. For products with Android, iOS, and web support, this can be very useful because you can primarily use the same code base for all platforms.

Additionally, NativeBase meets all of the criteria defined in the first subsection of this section. The following features are included in NativeBase:

- **Excellent theming support**: NativeBase also has very good theming support. Essentially, it works quite similarly to React Native Paper. You can easily change and extend the default themes and use them all over your app. It also supports light and dark modes out of the box.

- **Type declarations**: All components and themes come with type declarations. You also have excellent documentation on how to extend these types when it comes to customizing themes or components.

- **Icons**: NativeBase comes with its own icons, which are based on `react-native-vector-icons` for plain React Native projects or `@expo/vector-icon` for Expo projects.

- **Over 30 pre-built components**: All components are highly customizable and easy to use.

- **Responsive support**: NativeBase has excellent responsive design support. This means you can adapt your views to different screen sizes with just a few additional properties on your components.

- **Accessibility**: Based on React Native ARIA, NativeBase provides accessibility support for all components. This means you can easily provide support for screen readers, ensure a good contrast ratio, and enable keyboard interactions for your app.

Additionally, NativeBase comes with a Figma file, which makes it an ideal starting point for creating your own design system with a design expert. All in all, it is a very good solution for creating a beautiful UI in record time.

For more information on NativeBase, please visit the official documentation at `https://docs.nativebase.io/`.

As already mentioned, there are a lot more open source UI libraries out there. Please check this list for the most popular ones:

- React Native UI Kitten

- React Native Elements

- Material Kit Pro React Native by creative-tim

- Nachos UI Kit for React Native

These UI libraries can save you a lot of time. But as you want to create an individual app experience for your users, you should only use them as a starting point. Fortunately, most of them are adaptive enough that you can use them to create your own design while using the battle-proven structure of the library.

As your projects grow, I would recommend extending the library of your choice with your own components. If you like and think you have something that can be interesting for others too, you can even give something back to the community by creating pull requests and extending the official library.

After looking at the UI libraries, in the next subsection, you'll get to know another useful tool. This is especially useful when working on large applications, where UI components are shared between different repositories and where some developers only work on the UI components. It is called **Storybook**.

Using Storybook for React Native

Storybook is very popular in the plain React world. It is a tool that renders all your components in predefined states, so you can have a look at them without having to start your real app and navigate to the location where they are used.

With Storybook, you write stories, which are then packed into a storybook. Each of these stories contains a component. It also defines the location within the storybook. The following code example shows what a story can look like:

```
import {PrimaryButton} from '@components/PrimaryButton;
export default {
  title: 'components/PrimaryButton,
      component: PrimaryButton,
};
export const Standard = args => (
  <PrimaryButton {...args} />
);
Standard.args = {
  text: 'Primary Button',
      size: 'large',
          color: 'orange',
};

export const Alert = args => (
  <PrimaryButton {...args} />
);
```

```
Alert.args = {
  text: 'Alert Button',
      size: 'large',
          color: 'red',
};
```

In the first line, the `PrimaryButton` component is imported. The following default export defines the location in the storybook and which component the story is related to. The `Standard` const and the `Alert` const are different states, and the `PrimaryButton` component will be rendered and shown in the storybook. The corresponding `args` define this state:

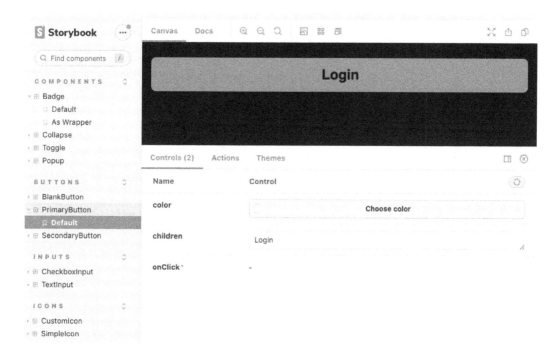

Figure 9.1 – Storybook running in a browser

Storybook on React Native either works on the iOS or Android simulator, a real device, or you can use React Native Web to create a web version of your components and render them into any browser. This is shown in *Figure 9.1* and can be especially useful when working with designers.

Storybook makes it possible to develop your components isolated from the rest of the application. It not only shows you the component, but it also lets you change the properties within a storybook. So, you can see how your component will behave in your real application under different circumstances.

I wouldn't use Storybook for small projects, but when your project and your team grow, Storybook can be a useful tool to increase your development speed on the UI part. This is especially the case when you have UI components that you share between different repositories. I would recommend this when you have multiple applications in your company that should all share the same look and feel.

In this case, a central repository for your components could be a good solution. With Storybook, this repository can be maintained by a developer and designer, without needing access to all your applications. You can read more about this in *Chapter 10, Structuring Large-Scale, Multi-Platform Projects*, in the *Writing own libraries* section.

For more information on Storybook, please visit the official documentation at `https://storybook.js.org/`.

Summary

In this chapter, you learned about useful tools for increasing code quality, catching the most common errors automatically, and speeding up the project setup along with the development process. You understood why type definitions are important and how to use ESLint and prettier to ensure your code meets certain criteria.

Additionally, you got to know the most popular React Native boilerplate solutions to start a project, and you learned what advantages and trade-offs each of these solutions have. At the end of the chapter, you learned about Storybook for React Native, how to use it, and in which scenarios it is a useful tool.

After learning about all these useful tools, it is time to dive deeper into large-scale projects. In the next chapter, you will learn how to set up and maintain a project structure, which will work for large-scale projects. Additionally, you will learn what options you have, to share code between different platforms, and which of these solutions works best in which scenario.

Part 3:
React Native in Large-Scale Projects and Organizations

You will learn how to use React Native in large organizations or large-scale projects. This includes structuring large applications, setting up good processes, using automation wherever possible, and starting to write your own libraries.

The following chapters are in this section:

- *Chapter 10, Structuring Large-Scale, Multiplatform Projects*
- *Chapter 11, Creating and Automating Workflows*
- *Chapter 12, Automated Testing of React Native Apps*
- *Chapter 13, Tips and Outlook*

10
Structuring Large-Scale, Multi-Platform Projects

I wholeheartedly believe that the structure of a software project is one of the key factors in deciding success or failure. This includes the application architecture, as well as the development process and the whole project organization.

The bigger the project is, the more developers that work on the project, and the longer a project runs, the more important it is to have a good project structure. But small projects can also fail because of a bad structure. So, most of this chapter is also applicable to smaller projects.

The project structure is especially important when using React Native to develop an application for multiple platforms, not only for iOS and Android. Different platforms have different needs and bring different user expectations. The best example to showcase this is the difference between iOS and Android and the web.

As already mentioned in *Chapter 4, Styling, Storage, and Navigation in React Native*, the concept of navigation in a mobile app and a web app is completely different. This is something you have to think about when planning the structure of your project.

The problem with investing in good architecture and a good project structure is that it always creates some overhead in the beginning. The following figure shows the dilemma:

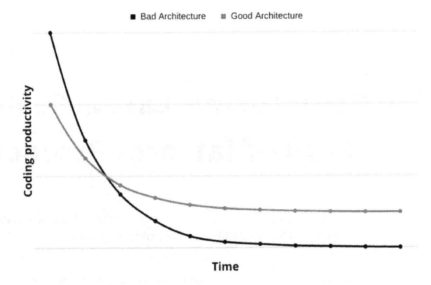

Figure 10.1 – Coding productivity reduces when the project grows over time

If you don't invest in your architecture in the beginning, you will start with higher productivity. If you invest in your architecture, you have to think about what should be achieved, in which direction the project could potentially develop, and what usage, team size, and requirements you will have when your project reaches maximum success.

These considerations take some time, and the implementation and execution of standardized processes may take even more time. It's always faster to just download a random template and start coding. But as stated before, it will pay off in the end, because with good application architecture and a good project structure, you will end up with software that's easy to maintain, test, and develop.

This is why you will learn about the following things in this chapter:

- Setting up an app architecture that works for large-scale enterprise projects
- Using React Native to deploy to different platforms
- Reusing code with your own libraries

Technical requirements

To be able to run the code in this chapter, you have to set up the following things:

- A working React Native environment (`bit.ly/prn-setup-rn` – React Native CLI Quickstart).

- You can find the example project in this repository: `https://bit.ly/prn-videoexample`.

- While most of this chapter should also work on Windows, I would recommend working on a Mac.

- This chapter contains some native code. You should have basic knowledge of Java or Kotlin and Objective-C or Swift for that.

Setting up an app architecture that works for large-scale enterprise projects

When we are talking about large-scale projects and how to set up a suitable app architecture, it makes sense to look at what's different in these large-scale projects compared to small-team or even single-developer projects.

The following points are the most important ones:

- **The project team is very big**: In large-scale projects, you usually have a big team with lots of developers. Often, these developers are scattered all over the world, which means they work in different time zones, have different first languages, and have completely different cultural backgrounds. That said, it is important to have a clear structure and clear responsibilities. Otherwise, your project will fail.

- **Multiple developers will work on the same part of the application**: At the latest stage when a deadline is approaching and a feature has to be finished, multiple developers will work on the same feature and the same part of the application. This means you should think about how to structure your code so that this is possible without having conflicts all the time.

- **Every error will be found by users**: In small projects with only a few users, it's likely that a lot of errors will never be found. In large-scale applications with a lot of users, it is nearly impossible that errors will remain unrevealed. This means you have to put in a lot more effort to find the errors yourself before releasing your application to the public.

- **The code has to be tested programmatically**: The larger the project is, and the longer a project runs, the more important it is to programmatically test your code. At some point, it is impossible to handle all testing manually. This means you must have an app architecture that supports this automated testing very well.

- **The code base will become very large**: As the term large-scale project already says, the project and its code base will become very large. This means you must provide a structure that makes it as easy as possible for new developers to understand what's going on in the project.

With these points in mind, we'll try to find some architectural approaches to support all of this.

Adapting our example project structure

The most important thing when the project grows is decomposition. This means you should try to split your components into small, meaningful segments wherever possible.

When we look at the project structure of our example project, we have already done a good job of decomposing our application, and the architecture we chose works fine for our use case. It already contains some things I would recommend keeping, even in large-scale projects. These are the following:

- **Using services**: Every API, SDK, or third-party connector should be wrapped in your own service. That enables you to change SDKs or even services and partners with minimal effort.

- **The separation between components and views**: Reusable components and navigable views should be kept in separate folders. This makes it easier for new developers to find the views they are working on.

However, this approach also brings some problems with it, especially when the code base grows and multiple developers work on it:

- Components and views are hard to test programmatically

- The component directory will grow really fast and become really big

- Single features will be hard to find and are scattered over the whole code base

- The code base as a whole will get quite confusing

- Multiple developers will have to touch the same files at the same time a lot

So, we'll make some adaptations to our approach. First, we'll take care of the component level. So far, we write our component with its business logic, UI, style, and types in one file. This will change now. We'll split our components into the following:

- `index.tsx`: The `index` file contains the business logic of the component such as data fetching, as well as the connection to the global application state. It only renders the following `.view` component.

- `<component>.view.tsx`: The `view` file contains the UI. It doesn't hold its own state nor does it connect directly to the global application state. It only renders the props it gets from the `index` file.

- `<component>.styles.tsx`: The `styles` file contains the React Native StyleSheet or the styled-components, depending on which approach you chose.

- `<component>.types.tsx`: The `types` file provides the data type for props and the state of the `index` and `view` files.

With this separation, we enable two things. First, it is much easier to have one developer work on the business logic and one on the UI, without creating merge conflicts or other problems. Second, our components now have much better support for automated testing.

We can use any component testing framework to render and test the views without having to mock our global state or our component state. And in addition to that, it's much easier to integrate tools such as Storybook with this approach.

To see that approach in action, you can have a look at the GitHub repository, choose the `chapter-10-split-home-view` tag, and check out the `views/home` folder.

> **Hint**
>
> To ensure that everyone sticks to this pattern and to make it simpler to create new views and components, you can use file generators. These are small scripts that use a template and typically a component name to create the structure you want to have. You can see an example in the GitHub repository. Choose the `chapter-10-generator` tag and have a look at the `util` folder. You can use the generator with `npm run generate <name>` to generate a new view.

After this change on the component level, we'll take a step back and look at the whole project again. The second change I would recommend when your project grows is to group your views and components by features. This makes it much easier to understand the whole project structure and navigate through the code.

I must admit that this depends on personal preferences and some people also like the clear separation between components and views even in large-scale projects, but I prefer the feature approach. This approach works as shown in the following figure:

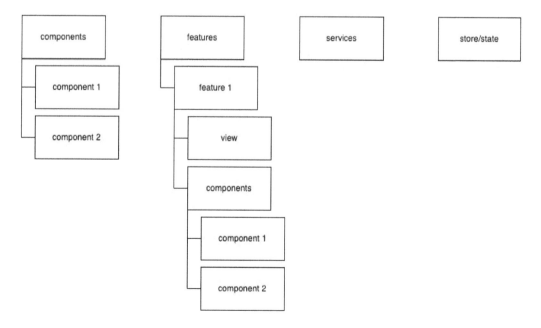

Figure 10.2 – A React Native feature-grouped architecture

This approach groups the application by features. It also has a component folder, which contains very basic general components such as buttons, lists, and avatars – basically, things that are used in every feature of your app to provide a consistent user experience. But every feature also has its own component folder where you can put components that you created only for this feature. There is also a modification of this approach, where you put multiple views in one feature.

From my personal experience, I can say that this feature approach makes the code base very clearly structured, and it makes it easier to find what you are searching for. On the other hand, you'll always have components where you are unsure whether you have to put them into the general components or not.

In the end, you'll have to find your own approach to how you want to structure your application. But in this section, you learned about the most important things you have to pay attention to in order to create a structure that works even when your project scales.

Now that you have learned how to structure a React Native project in general, we'll go a step further and focus on going multi-platform.

Using React Native to deploy to different platforms

In this section, you'll learn how to set up your React Native project to be able to support multiple platforms. Since it is the most common use case, we'll focus a lot on the web here, but the tips and approaches of these sections are also applicable to other platforms such as desktops and TVs.

When creating an application for multiple platforms, there are always two goals. First, you want to support as many platform-specific features as possible and want to give users the look and feel they are used to on this platform. Second, you try to have as much shared code as possible because this makes it easier to maintain and develop your application.

At first sight, these goals seem to be concurrent but there are intelligent ways to get the best of both worlds. Let's start with the simplest approach.

Using react-native-web to create a clone for web

When creating your application with React Native, you can use a library called `react-native-web` to run your React Native app on the web.

Before we start, you have to understand what `react-native-web` does. Basically, it maps all React Native components to HTML components. For example, a `<View/>` component will get `<div/>`. It also maps the native API calls of React Native to use the browser APIs wherever available. This means you'll get a plain React application for the web.

While `react-native-web` is a great library, it is not that easy to get started with it because you have to set up a separate build process to use it. This build process will create a standalone React web application. Like every React web application, it needs a bundler to create optimized browser-readable JavaScript code. A very popular solution is Webpack, which we will use for our web app as well. Also, every web application needs an entry point. In most cases, this is an `index.html` file, which then loads the JavaScript bundle that contains the React application. So, we'll have to add this to our project.

The whole process of setting up web support is described in a very detailed manner in the `react-native-web` documentation (which you can see here: `https://bit.ly/prn-rn-web`), but at the time of writing, this documentation is missing TypeScript support.

So, I'll describe the most important thing while we set up basic web support for our example application. You can find the complete working setup in the GitHub repository when choosing the `chapter-10-web` tag.

Installing react-native-web

We'll start with adding `react-native-web` and `react-dom` to our project. Please use the correct version of `react-dom`. Since we are using React 17 in our React Native app, we'll have to use `react-dom@17`. These libraries are necessary to create the React app. The installation can be done via npm:

```
npm install react-dom@17 react-native-web
```

Otherwise, it can be done via `yarn`:

```
yarn add react-dom@17 react-native-web
```

Now that we have installed `react-native-web`, we'll need to handle the build process and the development environment for the web.

Installing webpack

To do so, we'll add Webpack, the corresponding CLI, and a Webpack extension called `webpack-dev-server`. This extension provides a built-in development server that supports live reloading while you develop your application.

The installation of these npm libraries can be done with the following npm command:

```
npm install -saveDev webpack webpack-cli webpack-dev-server
```

Otherwise, you can use a `yarn` command:

```
yarn add --dev webpack webpack-cli webpack-dev-server
```

In addition to this basic Webpack setup, we'll also install two loaders. Loaders are a core concept of Webpack. They enable you to preprocess files and decide how they should be used in your bundle. We'll make use of the following loaders:

- `ts-loader`: This is a loader that preprocesses our TypeScript files and converts them to browser-readable JavaScript
- `file-loader`: This loader copies our asset binaries such as images in our final bundle

The last thing we need for our web build process to work is `html-webpack-plugin`. This plugin creates our entry point. It writes an `index.html` by loading an HTML template and adding the created JavaScript bundle.

These additions can be installed with the following npm command:

```
npm install -saveDev file-loader ts-loader html-webpack-plugin
```

Otherwise, install with the following `yarn` command:

```
yarn add --dev file-loader ts-loader html-webpack-plugin
```

Now that we have installed all tools, we have to configure our project.

Configuring the React Native project to work for web

First, let's create a JavaScript entry point for our application. To do so, we'll create `index.web.js` in the root folder of the application. This contains the following code.

```
AppRegistry.registerComponent(appName, () => App);
AppRegistry.runApplication(appName, {
  initialProps: {},
  rootTag: document.getElementById('movie-root'),
});
```

We use React Native `AppRegistry` to load our `<App />` component via the `registerComponent` function and then run our application with `runApplication`.

`runApplication` needs an HTML node as `rootTag` for the web. This HTML node will be replaced with the React application during `runApplication`. In our case, we'll get the element with the `movie-root` ID from the HTML document.

Next, we'll create a web/ folder in the root folder of our project. In this folder, we'll put an index. html template with the following content (please refer to the GitHub repository for the complete file):

```
<head>
  <title>
    Movie Application
  </title>
  <style>
      html, body { height: 100%; }
      body { overflow: hidden; }
      #movie-root { display:flex; height:100%; }
  </style>
</head>
<body>
  <div id="movie-root"></div>
</body>
```

In the head of the document, we define a title and some styles. The styles are important for the react-native-web application to show. The body only contains an empty <div /> with the #movie-root ID. This is the container we use in our JavaScript entry point.

Next, we'll have to configure our Webpack builder. To do so, please create webpack.config.js in the web/ folder. The following code snippet shows the most important configurations. For the complete file, please look at the GitHub repository:

```
const rootDir = path.join(__dirname, '..');
module.exports = {
  entry: {
    app: path.join(rootDir, './index.web.ts'),
  },
  output: {
    path: path.resolve(rootDir, 'dist'),
    filename: 'app-[hash].bundle.js',
  },
  module: {
    rules: [{
        test: /\.(tsx|ts|jsx|js)$/,
        exclude: /node_modules/,
        loader: 'ts-loader'
```

```
    }]
    },
  plugins: [
    new HtmlWebpackPlugin({
      template: path.join(__dirname, './index.html'),
    })
  ],
  resolve: {
    extensions: [
      '.web.tsx','.web.ts','.tsx','.ts','.js'
    ],
    alias: Object.assign({
      'react-native$': 'react-native-web',
    }),
  },
};
```

Let's work through this configuration from top to bottom. First, we defined our JavaScript entry point. Here, we put the `index.web.js` file we just created. Then, we defined our output. In this case, it's the `dist/` directory and a JS bundle with a hash value in the name to ensure that we have new filenames with every new build to prevent browser caching issues.

In the `module` section, we can define rules for which loaders should be used to preprocess which files. We use a Regex to test the filenames against and define loaders for all matching files. In this example, we use `ts-loader` for all files that include `.tsx`, `.ts`, `.jsx`, or `.js`, except everything in the `node_modules` folder.

In the next section of the file, we defined which plugins we'll use. In our case, it's only `HTMLWebpackPlugin` to create our entry point `index.html` from our template HTML file. The last part of the `config` file is the `resolve` section. Here is where the magic of the transformation of a React Native to a plain React web application is happening.

By creating the `react-native-web` alias for `react-native`, we replace all occurrences of `react-native` with `react-native-web`. This means all imports that were fetched from `react-native` are now fetched from `react-native-web`.

Now that our build process for the web application works, we'll have to make some small adaptations in our TypeScript setup:

```
"lib": ["es2017", "dom"],
"jsx": "react",
"noEmit": false,
```

We added dom to the lib section, changed the jsx mode to react, and switched noEmit from true to false. This is necessary to create the files in a way that Webpack can handle. With this step, the setup is complete.

Running the React Native code as a React app in the browser

Now, we can start our React Native app as a React web application in dev mode from the command line. You can do so with the following command:

```
cd web && webpack-dev-server
```

The following screenshot shows our example movie app running in the browser:

Figure 10.3 – Our example movie app running in the browser

Figure 10.3 shows the UI of the example movie app running in the browser. It works perfectly fine, running on the same code base as the native app. When you inspect the HTML with the browser's inspection tools, you'll see that all React Native components were transformed into HTML components.

As a final step of this section and to make development and creating production builds easier, we add two commands to the `scripts` section of `package.json`:

```
"start:web": "cd web && webpack-dev-server",
"build:web": "cd web && webpack",
```

The first line is the command we just used to start our application in `dev` mode. The second line is to build the application in production mode for deployment. This writes the complete bundle to the `dist` folder, as we defined in `webpack.config.js`.

In this subsection, you learned how to create a clone of your React Native app for the web. While this may work in some cases, most of the time, this isn't enough. User expectations between web and mobile are different in most areas and you also may want to use different libraries for web and mobile that don't support the other platform. A very easy solution for differentiating between different platforms is to make use of file endings.

Working with .native and .web file endings

As described in the previous subsection, we have two completely different build processes for web and native apps. While we configured our Webpack bundler to support `.web.ts` or `.web.tsx` files, the native Metro bundler supports `.native.ts` or `.native.tsx` files out of the box. This means that we can write platform-specific code by simply creating two versions of a file:

- `App.tsx` and `App.native.tsx` would result in our web application using `App.tsx` and our native application using `App.native.tsx`

- `App.tsx` and `App.web.tsx` would result in our web application using `App.web.tsx` and our native application using `App.tsx`

This approach can be used to share most of the code but make platform-specific versions of components. It can also be used to define different navigation stacks for the different platforms or use different navigation libraries by creating platform-specific `App.tsx` files.

All in all, this approach is quite powerful but has some limits. For example, you'll have to use the same versions of libraries you share between the platforms because both platforms share one `package.json` file. If you want to go one step further, you could either work with multiple packages in a `monorepo` or create your own libraries from the code you want to share, which you then import into different platform-specific projects.

Let's have a look at the `monorepo` approach first.

Working with multiple packages in a monorepo

For structuring your multi-platform React Native app as a `monorepo`, I recommend using `yarn` workspaces. This is a way to set up multiple JavaScript packages in a single repository. `yarn` optimizes the libraries in terms of versions and storage. It also allows the packages to be linked together, which is the main reason why we are using it here.

For more information on `yarn` workspaces, you can have a look at the official documentation (`https://bit.ly/prn-yarn-workspaces`). The following figure shows the structure of a multi-platform `monorepo` with `yarn` workspaces:

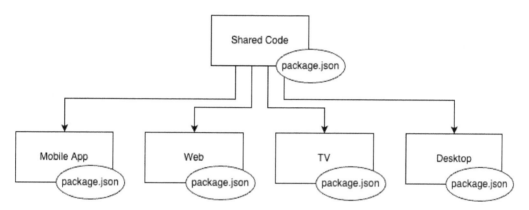

Figure 10.4 – A multi-platform React Native monorepo based on workspaces

You have the **Shared Code** package (often also called **App**), which can contain most parts of your application such as views, store, services, and components. This package isn't started directly and has no native or web entry point. Then, you have one package for every platform.

Each of these packages has its own `package.json` file and can define its own libraries and versions. This setup even allows you to use different versions of the same library on different platforms, as long as your shared code supports all of them.

The platform-specific packages contain the entry points, and I would also recommend putting platform-specific things such as navigation and the general application structure (layer stack or navigation tree) here. This makes it possible to not only create a clone of the same application for every platform but also to use very different approaches.

You could, for example, have a completely different layer stack on the web and mobile. This makes total sense because most of the time there are completely different needs for the different platforms. Some things you need on the web you don't even want to have on your mobile app and vice versa.

And there is another advantage of this package approach. There are a lot of frameworks based on React that perform a lot of web-specific optimizations such as supporting server-side rendering, adding browser history support to routing, or extensive web bundle optimizations. The most popular frameworks of this kind are **Next.js** and **Gatsby**. With this setup, you can use them for the web.

If you want to start with this `monorepo` setup, I can recommend an excellent template that you can find here: `https://bit.ly/prn-rn-universal-monorepo`. This template not only supports mobile and the web but also a couple of other frameworks and platforms such as Next.js, Electron, desktop, and even browser extensions. There is also a good description that guides you through the setup process, which you can find here: `https://bit.ly/prn-rn-anywhere`.

With this approach, we created different packages for different platforms for the first time. In this scenario, we only used a single repository, because that makes development quite easy. We just have to clone the repository, install the dependencies, and we are ready to go.

I really like this approach, but when the code base and the team grow a lot, it definitely makes sense to go one step further. To create a clearer separation of the different parts of the application with clear responsibilities, you can split the application into different projects. This means you will create your own libraries.

Reusing code with your own libraries

There are many good reasons to create your own library. Sharing code between different projects for different platforms is definitely one of them. But with your own library, you can also achieve the following things:

- **Ensure consistent design in all your applications**: When you are working in a company that provides multiple applications, it's a good idea to create a UI library that provides UI components for all these applications. This ensures a consistent design system.

- **Simplify backend connection**: You can extract your services to a library, which can then be used in all your projects. This ensures a unified backend connection layer.

- **Define responsibilities**: Every library can be maintained by its own maintainer or team. With this library approach, you can define clear responsibilities.

- **Provide additional functionality**: You can also write your own library to provide native functionality that isn't available in the way you need it from any community module. In this case, I would always recommend providing this functionality in the form of its own library (and making it available to the community if possible).

> **Notice**
>
> Most of the community modules out there started because someone had a problem that hadn't been solved. If you are in a position to be able to solve a problem with a new library or module, I would highly recommend sharing it with the community. Even if you don't want to do it for altruistic reasons, it can be a very good thing. Often, you can find others that share the same challenges and you can create a better solution together.

Creating our own library can be quite challenging. You can find a lot of tutorials and blog posts online on how to create the perfect setup for your own library. Some of them are good – some of them are bad. But instead of using one of them, I recommend a wrapper of tools called `react-native-builder-bob`.

Using react-native-builder-bob to write, maintain, and publish our own libraries

This tool makes the process of writing, maintaining, and publishing your own library very easy. It is created and maintained by a company called **Callstack**, which is very active in the React Native community and even contributes to the core of React Native.

They use `react-native-builder-bob` for their own libraries and a lot of the most popular libraries also do.

You can start creating your own library with `react-native-builder-bob` preconfigured using this simple command:

```
npx create-react-native-library <your-library-name>
```

This command will start the setup process and guide you through it with a couple of questions. The following screenshot shows this process:

```
●  ●  ●   professional-rn-code — node ‹ npm exec create-react-native-library test-library __CFBundleId...
alexanderkuttig@MacBook-Pro professional-rn-code % npx create-react-native-library test-library
Need to install the following packages:
  create-react-native-library@0.23.3
Ok to proceed? (y) y
✓ What is the name of the npm package? … react-native-test-library
✓ What is the description for the package? … Test
✓ What is the name of package author? … Alexander Kuttig
✓ What is the email address for the package author? … alexander.kuttig@horizon-alpha.com
✓ What is the URL for the package author? … https://www.horizon-alpha.com
✓ What is the URL for the repository? … https://www.github.com/alexkuttig/react-native-test-library
? What type of library do you want to develop? › - Use arrow-keys. Return to submit.
    Turbo module with backward compat (experimental)
    Turbo module (experimental)
    Native module
    Native view
›   JavaScript library
```

Figure 10.5 – Creating your own library with create-react-native-library

After answering questions about the author and the package, which are needed to create the `package.json`, `create-react-native-library` will ask you what type of library you want to develop.

You can choose between the following options:

- **Native module/Native view**: You should choose this if your module contains native code. These options use the current bridge architecture to communicate between JavaScript and native.

- **JavaScript library**: You should choose this if your module does not contain any native code. Most use cases such as simple UI libraries, service SDKs, and state providers fall in this category. Also, this is the correct type when you use other libraries that contain native code but your own library is a JavaScript-only library.

- **Turbo module**: At the time of writing, this type is in the experimental phase. This creates a native module based on the new React Native architecture (see the *Introducing the new React Native architecture* section from *Chapter 3, Hello React Native*).

We'll start by creating a JavaScript-only library. Imagine that we created our example application as one of many applications for a huge corporation. Because the management likes the design, they want all future applications to be able to stick to our design system. Therefore, we want to provide our `StyleConstants` file in our own library as the first step in setting up our corporate design system.

Creating a JavaScript-only library

To start our own JavaScript-only library, we'll choose **JavaScript library** from the `create-react-native-library` dropdown. `create-react-native-library` creates our library with a set of preconfigured tools, predefined scripts, a simple multiply function as the source, and even an example application to showcase the library. If you want to see a working example, you can have a look at the GitHub repository here: `https://bit.ly/prn-repo-styles-library`.

When we check the `root` folder of our newly created library, we'll find a lot of files we already know from our application. There is a `babel.config.js` file to define how Babel should transform our code, a `package.json` file, which contains information about the package, as well as all dependencies and scripts, and there is a `tsconfig.json` file, which contains all the information for the TypeScript compiler.

Next, we'll have a deeper look at `package.json`. Besides all the predefined information and configuration, I want to point out two important things. The first one is the information about where to find which parts of our library. This is what you see in the following code snippet:

```
"main": "lib/commonjs/index",
"types": "lib/typescript/index.d.ts",
"source": "src/index",
```

While we are creating our library in TypeScript, it will be compiled to pre-ES6 JavaScript by react-native-builder-bob, so that it will work in every React Native project, no matter what stack it is using (TypeScript, Flow, Plain JS, or Expo). This means the code of our library ships in different ways. That's what's defined in the following properties:

- main: This is the main entry point of your library. When you import anything from your library, this is the path where your project will look for exports.

- types: Since we are using TypeScript react-native-builder-bob creates types for our code so that everyone who uses typed JavaScript can work with the types we created.

- source: This is where the uncompiled source code can be found.

While we are only working in the source directory, the projects that use our library will only work with main and types.

The second thing I want you to have a look at is the scripts section, above all the following scripts.

```
"scripts": {
  "prepare": "bob build",
  "release": "release-it",
},
```

These scripts are the most essential part of this library setup. With the prepare script, you can run the build command of react-native-builder-bob. It will compile your library and provide the entry points you have just learned about.

The release script will use the release-it library to create a new release of your library. This initiates a guided process that will do the following things:

- Update the library version
- Create a changelog
- Publish your library to npm
- Commit the library version update to git
- Add a git tag
- Push the changes to the remote repository
- Create a release on GitHub

This script is very useful because it forces you to stick to best practices in terms of releasing and tagging your library.

Now that you know how the library project is structured, let's use this library to publish our styles. Since we already collected all our style information in our StyleConstants file, this is simple.

Go to the `src/index.tsx` file of the library project and paste the contents of the `StyleConstants.ts` file. Next, commit the changes and build and publish the library with the following command:

```
npm run prepare && npm run release
```

> **Notice**
>
> You need to create a free account at `https://www.npmjs.com/` and log in from the command line with `npm login` to be able to publish your library.

After you publish your library package, you can install it in your project. You can use the regular npm command:

```
npm install <your-library-name>
```

Alternatively, you can use the `yarn` command:

```
yarn add <your-library-name>
```

Now that you are able to access your styles via your library, you can delete your `StyleConstants.ts` file and replace all imports with your library. The following figure shows the change for `Home.styles.tsx`:

```
2  import {                                    2  import {
3    ColorConstants,                           3    ColorConstants,
4    FontConstants,                            4    FontConstants,
5    SizeConstants,                            5    SizeConstants,
6- } from '../../constants/StyleConstants';  → 6+ } from 'prn-video-example-styles';
```

Figure 10.6 – Importing a change from a local file to a library

As you can see, the imports stay the same, only the `from` path changes to the library. You have to do this in all files where you used `StyleConstants`.

As you learned in this subsection, the process of creating your own library is quite complex, but it gets a lot easier when you work with the right tools. But since our example was a JavaScript-only library, it was the easiest type of React Native library. It gets more complex when adding native code to your library.

Understanding the difference between native libraries

As you already know, React Native has a JavaScript part and a native part. This means we can make use of native platform-specific code when we want to. This not only works with app projects but also with libraries. Native code is written in platform-specific languages such as Kotlin or Java for Android or Swift or Objective-C for iOS.

But it isn't only the language that differs from platform to platform. The process of how the application manages its third-party packages and how to build and deploy is completely different.

Android uses Gradle to fetch packages and build your app. For iOS, there are multiple package managers but React Native relies heavily on CocoaPods. The build is done via Xcode.

This means when you are adding native code to your library, you not only have to deliver and import your JavaScript code but you also have to provide the native code and add it to the native build process that gets included in the native bundle.

With this setup, your native code also gets included in your library bundle. To be able to write native code, you have to choose `Native Module` when creating your library with `create-react-native-library`. This will create two additional folders (`android` and `ios`) that contain the native code, as well as the configuration files for the native build process.

For Android, this is a `build.gradle` file, which can be found in the `android` folder. For iOS, this is a `.podspec` file, which can be found in the `root` folder of the library.

All these files are created for you, so you shouldn't need to change them. When installing your library with native code, React Native autolinking will take care of everything for you on Android. On iOS, you'll have to run `npx pod-install` to include the native part of your library in the native project.

Now that you are able to create pure JavaScript libraries and libraries with native code, we'll take another look at how to provide them. We used the public npm registry to host our library as a public package.

While I really like the approach of sharing everything with the community, you may have the requirement to keep your libraries private, especially when they are important parts of corporate applications. The next subsection will show you how to only provide access to your libraries to selected people.

Setting access restrictions on libraries

There are some ways to share your library only with selected people. These two are the most common ones:

- **Use a paid npmjs.com plan**: You can define permissions on your packages when using a paid `npmjs.com` plan. This means that only people you explicitly allow will have access to your package.

- **Import your packages directly from the repository**: You don't need to use `https://www.npmjs.com/` to import your packages. You can also import packages directly from your repository. This would look as follows in your `package.json`:

  ```
  "prn-video-example-styles": "git+https://github.com/
  alexkuttig/video-example-styles"
  ```

- You could even specify tags, branches, or commits your package should be fetched from by adding a # symbol followed by the tag name, branch name, or commit hash.

Again, I would highly recommend publishing your modules and not keeping them private wherever possible. This community with thousands of well-maintained public packages is one of the main reasons why React Native is so successful. So, giving something back to the community is always a good idea.

Summary

In this chapter, you learned how to structure large-scale or multi-platform products. You are now able to create a project structure that works for large-scale and long-running projects.

You also created a clone of your example React Native mobile app on the web and understood why this isn't always the best idea. You then learned how to create multi-platform applications that meet user expectations while keeping a high percentage of shared code.

In the last section of this chapter, you learned how to create, release, and maintain your own libraries, what the difference between JavaScript-only libraries and libraries with native code is, and how to only publish these libraries to selected people.

After focusing on creating a good structure for the code base itself, in the next chapter, we'll focus on how to implement well-working processes and how to support these processes with **Continuous Integration (CI)** tools.

11
Creating and Automating Workflows

Automating workflows with modern workflow automation is an absolute must in large-scale projects. It will save you a lot of time, but even more importantly, it will guarantee that you don't miss anything and your repetitive processes for steps such as checking for code styling and code quality, building your application, or releasing your application just work.

Next, it gives you the confidence that the code you have just written doesn't only work on your machine because it is cloned and started on a clean machine. Last, it ensure the project isn't dependent on individual people.

In particular, steps such as building and releasing an application can become quite complex in larger-scale projects, so not every member of the project can do it. But with the correct automation setup, all it takes is the push of a button.

When talking about workflow automation, you'll also often hear the terms **continuous integration** (**CI**) and **continuous delivery** (**CD**). Both terms describe automated workflows. CI refers to the development phase of a project. This means that every developer integrates the code they create into a shared repository frequently, normally multiple times a day. In every integration, the code is checked automatically (TypeScript/Flow, ESLint, Prettier, and Tests) and the developer gets immediate feedback. DS refers to the deployment or delivery step. It describes the automation of building and delivering the application.

Since CI is possible when building apps, you should use it. CD works for testing builds, but for public production builds, such as mobile apps, it doesn't work well. Releasing to the public multiple times a day isn't possible because every release has to be reviewed manually by Apple and Google to be available in the respective app store.

And even if it were possible (which you could achieve using CodePush, as you'll learn in *Chapter 13, Tips and Outlook*) I wouldn't recommend pushing updates too frequently as it will result in every user having to update the app version on every start.

That's why we will focus on CI for development and building automated workflows for the build and release step, which can either be triggered manually for public production builds or automatically for internal testing builds (CD).

This enables you to deliver your application updates automatically to your test users and ship your app to the public with the push of a button while not annoying your real users with too frequent updates.

Since the best automation tools are worth nothing when the workflows you automate are not good, we'll also focus on creating an effective development workflow in this chapter.

In this chapter, we will cover the following topics:

- Understanding integration/delivery workflow automation
- Creating a collaborative development workflow
- Creating useful CI pipelines for the development process
- Understanding workflow automation and CD for build and release

Technical requirements

To be able to run the code in this chapter, you must set up the following:

- A working React Native environment (`bit.ly/prn-setup-rn` – React Native CLI Quickstart)
- While most of this chapter should also work on Windows, I recommend working on a Mac
- An account with GitHub to run the CI pipelines
- An account with Bitrise to run the Bitrise delivery workflows

Understanding integration/delivery workflow automation

The process of integration and delivery workflow automation is pretty simple: you need a repository and an automation tool or build server that can connect to your repository. Then, you must define rules regarding which Git events should send information to the server to trigger certain scripts. The following diagram illustrates this process:

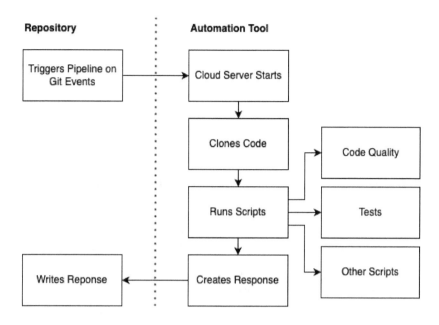

Figure 11.1 – Basic CI setup

A Git event such as commit, pull request, or merge triggers the automation tool. The automation tool starts a clean server with a configuration defined in the automation tool settings. Then, it clones the code from your repository and starts running scripts on it. When it comes to React Native apps, these scripts normally start with installing all the project dependencies and running static type checkers (Flow/TypeScript).

Next, you should run code quality tools such as ESLint and Prettier and check whether the code matches all the requirements. Most of the time, you would also run some tests here (more on this in *Chapter 12, Automated Testing of React Native Apps*).

You can run every other script here, as well as integrating other cloud tools such as SonarQube (`https://bit.ly/prn-sonarcube`, an advanced code quality tool) or Snyk (`https://bit.ly/prn-snyk`, a cloud-based security intelligence tool).

After the scripts have been executed, your automation tool creates a response and sends it back to your repository. This answer then gets shown in your repository and can be used to allow or deny further actions.

Nowadays, basic automation tools are integrated into all popular Git-based source code repository services, including GitHub (GitHub Actions), Bitbucket (Bitbucket Pipelines), and GitLab (GitLab CI/CD). While these tools work fine for React Native CI requirements, building and deploying mobile apps is a very complex process with special requirements.

For example, iOS apps can still only be built on macOS machines. While this step is technically also possible with most of these basic automation tools, I wouldn't recommend using them for building and deploying.

For this step, there is a special toolkit called fastlane that integrates into special workflow automation tools such as Bitrise, CircleCI, and Travis CI. I recommend using the toolkit as it will save you a lot of hours.

Now that you've learned about the theory behind process automation, it's time to think about what our development process should look like. We need a good process in place before we can automate anything.

Creating a collaborative development workflow

In large-scale projects, one of the most important things is up-to-date information. Typically, in those projects, a lot of people have to be coordinated and multiple project parts have to work together to build a complex product. While information is important, it shouldn't limit development speed.

So, we have to create a workflow that can be supported with automation to fulfill both requirements. The following diagram shows the important parts of this workflow:

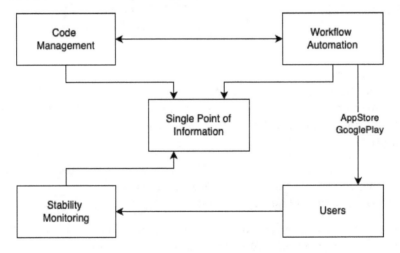

Figure 11.2 – Workflow automation setup

As you can see, four technical parts are needed for the workflow. These are as follows:

- **Single Point of Information**: All information is centralized here. Normally, this is an issue tracker where every task, bug, or feature request is created as an issue. Examples include Jira, ClickUp, GitLab issues, and GitHub issues.

- **Code Management**: This is where your source code is stored. It should be able to integrate with your *Single Point of Information* to transfer information about which issues have already been finished or worked on. Examples include Bitbucket, GitHub code, and GitLab repository.

- **Workflow Automation**: This is where your application gets tested and built. This tool should also be able to communicate with your *Single Point of Information* to transfer information about the state of the issues. Examples include Bitbucket Pipelines, GitHub Actions, GitLab CI/CD, CircleCI, and Bitrise.

- **Stability Monitoring**: After your app has been deployed to your users, you should track information about its stability. Crashes or other problems should be automatically reported to your *Single Point of Information*. Examples include Bugsnag, Sentry, Rollbar, and Crashlytics. You will learn more about these tools in *Chapter 13, Tips and Outlook*.

Now, we can start creating our development workflow. The following diagram shows the standard feature branch workflow that I recommend using:

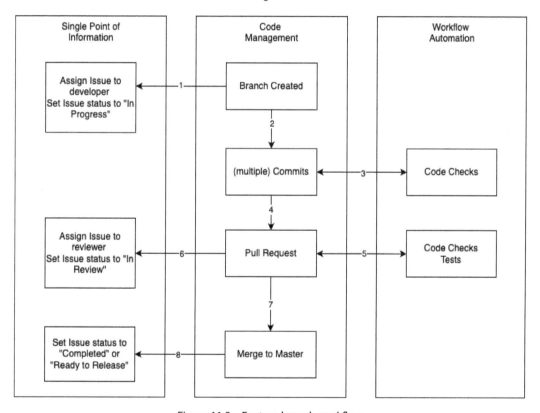

Figure 11.3 – Feature branch workflow

As the workflow's name suggests, for every feature (which can also be a bug or improvement – here, every single issue is considered a feature) a new branch is created. Then, the following workflow starts:

1. When the branch is created, the single point of information must be updated so that it contains information regarding whether the issue has already been worked on and who is working on it.

2. Next, the developer makes one or multiple commits to solve the issue.

3. Every commit is checked by the workflow automation tool.

4. If there are errors, the developer will be notified immediately. When the developer thinks they have solved the issue and finished their work, they create a pull request (sometimes called a **merge request**).

5. This pull request is also checked by the workflow automation, but this time, not only with simple checks but with more extensive ones (for example, E2E tests).

6. If everything passes, the single point of information must be updated. The issue gets assigned to another developer for review and the status is changed to reflect the review status.

7. If changes are requested, the process falls back to *Step 1*. If the reviewer is satisfied with the result, they can merge the code to the master or main branch.

8. Again, the single point of information has to be updated, to reflect the correct status of the issue.

I like this process a lot because it provides you with a lot of things you need. Some of these are as follows:

- You always know the exact state of the project.

- Most parts of the workflow can be automated to save time. Normally, the developers and reviewers only have to work in the code management tool; everything else is automated.

- It ensures that every code is double-checked by another developer, which increases code quality.

- The reviewer doesn't have to do checks for basic code quality because that's done automatically.

Now that we know our process, let's start writing the automation pipelines.

Creating useful CI pipelines for the development process

Again, we'll use our example project here. First, we'll set up a pipeline that can support us during the development process with very simple checks for *Step 3* of *Figure 11.3*. We'll use GitHub Actions to execute this CI pipeline, but it works very similar with Bitbucket (`https://bit.ly/prn-bitbucket-pipelines`) and GitLab CI/CD (`https://bit.ly/prn-gitlab-cicd`).

First, we have to create the scripts we want to use in our pipelines. In our example, we want to run type checking with the TypeScript compiler and static code analysis with ESLint and Prettier to ensure the correct code styling is in place.

For this, we'll provide the following scripts in the `scripts` section of our `package.json` file:

```
"typecheck": "tsc --noEmit",
"lint": "eslint ./src",
"prettier": "prettier ./src --check",
```

Next, we have to create a workflow file that can be interpreted by GitHub Actions. Since this is a fully integrated workflow automation, as soon as we push this file to our GitHub repository, GitHub Actions starts working.

This is what our first workflow automation pipeline (or CI pipeline) looks like. You have to create it under `.github/workflows/<the github actions workflow name>.yml`:

```
name: Check files on push
on: push

jobs:
  run-checks:
    runs-on: ubuntu-latest
    steps:
        - uses: actions/checkout@v2
        - name: install modules
          run: npm install
        - name: run typecheck
          run: npm run typecheck
        - name: run prettier check for code styling
          run: npm run prettier
        - name: run eslint check for code errors
          run: npm run lint
```

Let's go through the code line by line. The first line defines the name of the workflow. The second line defines when the workflow should run. In this case, we want to run it on every push to the repository, no matter to which branch or from which author this push comes.

> **Hint**
>
> You can run workflows on different trigger events. You can find the full list in the documentation (`https://bit.ly/prn-github-actions-events` for the GitHub Actions event list).
>
> Some especially useful events for the development process described in the previous section are push and pull requests. You can also limit these triggers to specific branches.

Next, you can see the `jobs` section. Here, you define the actual workflow, which contains one or multiple jobs that can run in sequence or parallel. In this case, we defined one job with multiple steps.

The first thing we have to do for our job is define which machine it should run on. Every workflow automation tool has a lot of predefined machine images you can choose from, but you can always provide your own machines to run the automation pipelines. In our example, we'll use the latest Ubuntu image that is provided by GitHub Actions.

Next, we define the steps of our job. This can either be a predefined action that we use with the `uses` command or an action that we create by ourselves. In our example, we make use of both options. First, we use a predefined action to check out our code, then we use four self-created actions to install the modules and run our checks.

> **Hint**
>
> When working with workflow automation tools, the time your workflows run for is the metric you will pay for. So, you should always think about how to structure your workflows so that you spend as little time as possible on the automation tool machines.

As soon as we pushed this file to our GitHub repository, the first run of the automated workflow was triggered. In this case, the machine started, cloned the repository, installed the dependency modules, and ran our checks. You can watch the automation running in the **GitHub Actions** tab.

In the preceding *Hint*, you learned that optimizing workflows to run as fast as possible is important. So, that's what we'll do next. The following diagram shows two ways to optimize our workflow so that we can complete it faster:

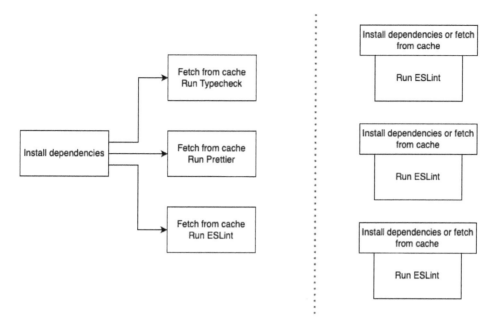

Figure 11.4 – Parallelize workflows

The easiest way to complete things faster is by running them in parallel. GitHub Actions doesn't allow you to run steps in parallel, but you can run multiple jobs in parallel. You have to investigate your workflow in detail to find out which parts can be parallelized, and which steps are better to run in sequence.

In our example, it wouldn't make much sense to just create three jobs for the three tasks. This is because the step that takes the most time installs the dependencies and it would be necessary for all three jobs. Fortunately, it is possible to work with caches so that we don't have to repeat cacheable tasks with any test run.

On the left-hand side of the preceding diagram, you can see the pipeline setup for our example, which installs dependencies first and then runs our three jobs in parallel. All three jobs fetch the dependencies from the cache, which is populated in the install step. On the right-hand side, you can see another setup. In this setup, we have three parallel jobs, running completely independently from each other.

All three jobs try to fetch the dependencies from the cache and install them only if they can't find them there. Both options are faster in certain scenarios. If you have to install the dependencies, the second setup would take a little longer because the install step will be triggered three times (because the steps start in parallel, and at the time they start, the dependencies are either cached or not for all three jobs).

The first setup only triggers the dependency install once and ensures that it is cached for the other jobs. This first setup will take more time in most scenarios because it requires you to run two jobs in sequence (*install + typecheck/Prettier/ESLint*).

This is why I recommend going with the second setup, as shown in the following code:

```
name: Check files on push alternative
on: push
jobs:
  typecheck:
    runs-on: ubuntu-latest
    steps:
      - uses: actions/checkout@v2
      - uses: actions/setup-node@v2
        with:
          node-version: '14'
      - uses: actions/cache@v2
        id: npm-cache
        with:
          path: '**/node_modules'
          key: ${{ runner.os }}-node-${{
              hashFiles('**/package-lock.json') }}
      - name: Install dependencies if not cached
        if: steps.npm-cache.outputs.cache-hit != 'true'
        run: npm install
      - name: run typecheck
        run: npm run typecheck
  prettier:
    runs-on: ubuntu-latest
    steps:
      - uses: actions/checkout@v2
      - uses: actions/setup-node@v2
        with:
          node-version: '14'
      - uses: actions/cache@v2
        id: npm-cache
        with:
          path: '**/node_modules'
          key: ${{ runner.os }}-node-${{
              hashFiles('**/package-lock.json') }}
      - name: Install dependencies if not cached
```

```
            if: steps.npm-cache.outputs.cache-hit != 'true'
            run: npm install
        - name: run prettier check for code styling
            run: npm run prettier
    lint:
      runs-on: ubuntu-latest
      steps:
        - uses: actions/checkout@v2
        - uses: actions/setup-node@v2
          with:
            node-version: '14'
        - uses: actions/cache@v2
          id: npm-cache
          with:
            path: '**/node_modules'
            key: ${{ runner.os }}-node-${{
                hashFiles('**/package-lock.json') }}
        - name: Install dependencies if not cached
          if: steps.npm-cache.outputs.cache-hit != 'true'
          run: npm install
        - name: run eslint check for code errors
          run: npm run lint
```

As you can see, the three jobs are very similar. We check out the project, set the node environment with a specified node version, and check the cache. The key of the cache contains the OS version of the runtime and the hash value of the package-lock.json file, which changes when anything changes with the dependencies (version updates, new libraries, and so on).

Next, we have a conditional install step, which only installs the dependencies when we didn't hit the cache. This is the case when the name of our cache changes, as described previously, or if the cache expires (which it does after it hasn't been used for at least 1 week).

Finally, we execute our typecheck/Prettier/ESLint step. While this parallelization seems to be quite complex, it can save you a lot of time when using it at scale. So, you should take some time to set up your workflow automation so that it fits your needs.

All modern code management solutions, such as GitHub, Bitbucket, and GitLab, have a very deep integration of workflow automation tools. This means that as soon as you have configured your workflow automation, you will see the results not only in the workflow automation tool or section but also in your repository. For example, it will show the result of every commit that was tested directly in the commit list.

For more details, you have to visit the workflow automation tool or section – in our case, GitHub Actions – to see the results of the CI pipeline. If everything worked as expected, you will see a green checkmark. If the workflow detected that an error was thrown in any of our checks, we will see a red dot, which notifies us about our failed workflow execution.

The following screenshot shows a list with multiple workflow runs:

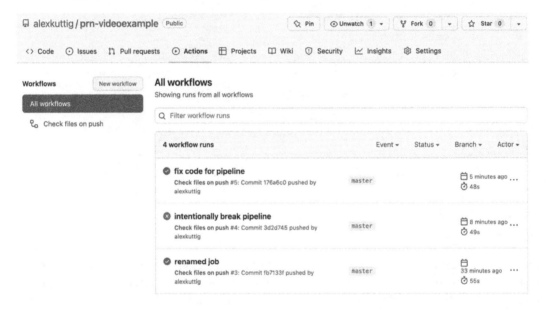

Figure 11.5 – Workflow runs inside GitHub Actions

In this example, two runs of our workflow succeeded, while one of them failed. The failed workflow run is always the interesting one because it provides a lot of information about what went wrong.

By clicking on it, you will see information about the logs and execution times so that you can find and fix the error. This is how it looks inside **GitHub Actions**:

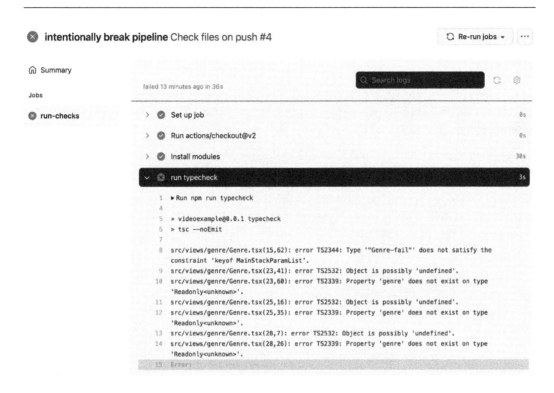

Figure 11.6 – Failed workflow run in GitHub Actions

As you can see, we don't only see which check fails, but also the detailed logs. In this case, we used the wrong type in the Genre.tsx file, which resulted in a bunch of errors. With this workflow, we didn't only find the error – we also know the exact file and line number where we have to fix our error.

> **Note**
>
> Working with CI pipelines is all about giving feedback as soon as possible. You should use tools such as Husky (https://bit.ly/prn-husky) to run your pipelines before committing them to your local machine. This not only replaces your workflow automation tool, but it can also be useful to shorten the feedback cycle even more.

Now that you know how to create CI pipelines to support and improve the development process, let's have a look at building and releasing apps.

Understanding workflow automation and CD for build and release

Before we start creating our pipeline, let's look at building and releasing apps in general. Android uses Gradle as its build tool and a KeyStore file to verify ownership of an app. If you are not familiar with releasing Android apps, please read this guide first: `https://bit.ly/prn-android-release`.

On iOS, you have to use Xcode to build, sign, and release your app. If you are not familiar with this process, please read this guide first: `https://bit.ly/prn-ios-release`.

Fortunately, for both platforms (Android and iOS), the build and deployment processes can be executed via command-line tools. Gradle works as a command-line tool itself and Xcode provides the Xcode command-line tools. This means we can write scripts for the complete process, which we can then invoke with our workflow automation tools.

Unfortunately, these processes are quite complex, so we don't want to write scripts by ourselves. This is where a toolset called **Fastlane** comes into play. Fastlane is a specialized automation tool for iOS and Android apps. It provides scripts for signing, building, and deploying code to the Apple App Store and Google Play. You can find more information about Fastlane here: `https://bit.ly/prn-fastlane`.

The reason why I do not recommend using Fastlane directly is that it has excellent integration with advanced workflow automation tools such as Bitrise and CircleCI. We'll take a deeper look at Bitrise as an example, but other tools such as CircleCI and Travis CI work very similarly.

Bitrise integrates into your code management solution the same way you saw with GitHub Actions. You can use certain events to trigger workflows. It provides an excellent UI to create these workflows. I like working with it because it is quite easy and saves a lot of time.

You can choose from a huge variety of predefined actions, which mainly focus on iOS and Android apps. Bitrise even provides its own automatic setup for React Native apps. The following diagram shows a typical iOS build and deploy workflow:

Figure 11.7 – Bitrise iOS build and deploy workflow

The steps are executed column after column. So, we start by activating an SSH key to be able to connect to the repository. Next, the repository gets cloned. After that, the npm dependency modules are installed, as well as the native module via CocoaPods.

As an example, for every other script that can be integrated here, we'll fetch the most recent translation files for our app UI to be integrated with the app bundle in the next step. Then, we'll update the version number inside our Info.plist file. Next, the workflow handles the code signing, builds the application, and deploys it to App Store Connect.

The workflow for an Android build looks pretty similar:

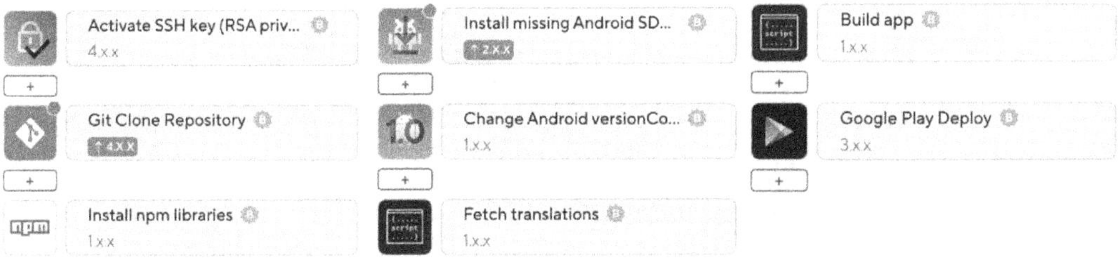

Figure 11.8 – Bitrise Android build and deploy workflow

Again, the actions are executed column after column. The first column is the same as in the iOS workflow. The SSH key gets activated, the repository gets cloned, and the npm dependency modules are installed. Next, we have to install all the missing Android SDK tools.

Then, we must change the Android version code and – as we did in iOS – fetch the translations to be bundled with the application. Then, we must build the application and deploy it to Google Play.

Under the hood, Bitrise and other CI tools with graphical workflow editors use the same logic you learned about while setting up the development CI pipeline. The following code is for the .yml file for the iOS workflow:

```
ios-release-build:
  steps:
  - activate-ssh-key@4:
      run_if: '{{getenv "SSH_RSA_PRIVATE_KEY" | ne ""}}'
  - git-clone@4: {}
  - npm@1:
      inputs:
      - command: install
  - cocoapods-install@2: {}
  - script@1:
      inputs:
      - content: |-
          cd scripts
          bash getTranslationsCrowdin.sh
```

```
    - set-ios-info-plist-unified@1:
        inputs:
        - bundle_version: „$VERSION_NUMBER_IOS"
        - info_plist_file: "$BITRISE_SOURCE_DIR_PLIST"
    - manage-ios-code-signing@1:
    - xcode-archive@4.3:
        inputs:
        - project_path: "$BITRISE_PROJECT_PATH"
        - distribution_method: app-store
        - export_method: app-store
    - deploy-to-itunesconnect-deliver@2:
```

As you can see, it has the same structure. It contains multiple steps, which can get additional input as configuration. Like any other workflow automation tool, Bitrise works with environment variables. These variables are stored on the platform and replace the placeholders (here, they start with $) during the execution of the workflow.

> **Note**
>
> You should never add private keys or signing information to your repository. If this happened, everyone who has access to the repository would get access to this private data and would be able to sign releases for your application. It's much better to store this information in your workflow automation tool because there, nobody can obtain the keys and signing certificates, but all developers with access can still create new releases.

This workflow can either be triggered manually, which I would recommend for public production builds, or automatically, which I would recommend for internal or public testing builds.

Summary

Now, it's time to wrap up this chapter. First, you learned what the terms workflow automation, continuous integration, and continuous delivery mean and which of them work for app development. Then, you considered a development process you can use in large-scale projects.

Next, you learned how to support this process through workflow automation with simple workflow automation tools such as GitHub Actions. Finally, you learned about specialized workflow automation tools such as Bitrise so that you can build, sign, and deploy your iOS and Android apps.

One topic that is especially important when it comes to workflow automation was left out in this chapter – **testing**. Automated testing is important during the development phase, as well as before shipping your releases. Therefore, we'll have a detailed look at automated testing in the next chapter.

12
Automated Testing for React Native Apps

Automating tests is one of the most important things you must do when your project grows. It can help ensure a certain level of quality of your application and can enable you to run faster release cycles without introducing bugs in every release. I recommend writing automated tests for your application as soon as possible.

It is much easier to start writing tests right from the beginning because then, you are forced to structure your code in a way that works for automated testing. It can be hard to refactor an application to use automated testing when this wasn't in focus at the beginning.

In this chapter, you will learn about automated testing in general and how to use automated testing in React Native apps. You will learn about the different tools and frameworks for different types of automated testing. These tools and frameworks are used in production by some of the most widely used apps in the world, so I recommend using them.

To give you a good overview of all these topics, this chapter will cover the following topics. If you are already familiar with automated testing in general, you can skip the first section:

- Understanding automated testing
- Working with unit and integration tests in React Native
- Working with component tests
- Understanding end-to-end tests

Technical requirements

To be able to run the code in this chapter, you must set up the following:

- A working React Native environment (`bit.ly/prn-setup-rn` – React Native CLI Quickstart).

- While most of this chapter should also work on Windows, I recommend working on a Mac. You need to work on a Mac to run Detox end-to-end tests on iOS simulators.

- An AWS account for accessing AWS Device Farm.

Understanding automated testing

There are different forms of automated testing. The following forms of automated testing are the most common ones and will be covered in this chapter:

- **Unit tests**: Unit tests cover the smallest parts of your business logic, such as single functions.

- **Integration tests**: This form of testing works very similar to unit tests in React Native, but it covers multiple pieces of your business logic and tests whether the integration of these parts works as expected.

- **Component tests**: These tests cover your React Native UI components and check whether they do what they are expected to do. You can also check for (unexpected) changes in your components with this form of testing.

- **End-to-end tests**: This form of testing simulates end user behavior and checks whether your whole application behaves like it is expected to do.

To get the most out of automated testing, you should implement all four types of tests. All of them cover different areas of your application and can help you find different types of errors that the other types of testing can't find.

When working with automated testing, you should try to have high **code coverage**. Code coverage describes the percentage of your code that is covered by your automated tests. While it is a good metric to get an idea of whether automated tests are used in a project and that you didn't forget any parts of your application, it has little significance on its own.

This is because it doesn't help to write one test for every line of code you have. When working with automated tests, especially unit tests, integration tests, and component tests, you should always write multiple tests for the part you want to test, covering the most common use cases as well as important edge cases. This means you have to think a lot before writing your tests.

With unit tests, integration tests, and component tests, you typically test small parts of your application. This also means you have to create an environment where these small parts can work on their own. This can be achieved by mocking dependencies that are used in the tested part.

Mocking means writing your own implementation of a dependency for the testing environment, to ensure it behaves as expected and to rule out that an error in the dependency leads to an error in the test.

> **Note**
>
> It's not always clear which parts of an application should be mocked in a test. I would recommend mocking more rather than less in unit tests because you want to test whether a very small part of your code behaves as it is expected to. In integration and component tests, I recommend mocking less rather than more because you want to test larger parts of your application and see whether the whole combination works.

Because unit tests, integration tests, and component tests run in a test environment and use only parts of your application, they are very reliable. There aren't many things that can interfere with these tests to distort the test results. This is different compared to working with end-to-end tests.

These tests run on your real application on a simulator or real device and depend on things such as network connectivity or other device behavior. This can lead to **test flakiness**. A flaky test is a test that passes and fails on different test runs without any code changes.

This is a real problem because it results in you having to manually check whether the test fails only because it is flaky or because it found a bug in your application. We'll cover test flakiness in more detail in the *Understanding end-to-end tests* section.

But first, we'll start by testing the business logic parts of our application automatically by using unit and integration tests.

Working with unit and integration tests in React Native

When you start a new React Native project, it comes with a testing framework called **Jest** preconfigured. This is the recommended framework for unit tests, integration tests, and component tests. We'll use it in the following sections.

Let's start with unit testing. We'll use our example project again, but we will go back a few commits to use the local movie service implementation. You can have a look at the complete code by selecting the `chapter-12-unit-testing` branch in the example repository.

This local service implementation is very suitable as an example for unit testing because it has no dependencies. We know the data it is working on and can write tests very easily. In this example, we'll test two API calls: `getMovies` and `getMovieById`.

The following code shows our first unit tests:

```
import {getMovies,getMovieById} from '../src/services/
movieService';
describe('testing getMovies API', () => {
```

```
test('getMovies returns values', () => {
  expect(getMovies()).toBeTruthy();
});
test('getMovies returns an array', () => {
  expect(getMovies()).toBeInstanceOf(Array);
});
test('getMovies returns three results', () => {
  expect(getMovies()).toHaveLength(46);
});
});
describe('testing getMovieById API', () => {
  test('getMovies returns movie if id exists', () => {
    expect(getMovieById(892153)).toBeTruthy();
  });
  test('getMovies returns movie with correct information,
  () => {
    const movie = getMovieById(892153);
    expect(movie?.title).toBe('Tom and Jerry Cowboy Up!');
    expect(movie?.release_date).toBe('2022-01-24');
  });
  test('getMovies returns nothing if id does not exist', ()
  => {
    expect(getMovieById(0)).toBeFalsy();
  });
});
```

The preceding code contains six tests grouped into two sections. The first section contains all tests regarding the getMovies API call. With the first test, we ensure that the getMovies call returns a value. The second test checks whether getMovies returns an array, while the last test validates that the returned array has the length we expect.

> **Note**
>
> You might be wondering why we need three tests here when the last one fails as soon as one of the first two fails. This is because it gives us useful information so that we can see which tests fail. This makes debugging and searching for changes or bugs a lot easier.

In the second section of the code example, we test the getMoviesById block. Again, we have three tests. The first one verifies that the API call returns a value for a movie ID we know exists. The second test checks that the correct movie is returned. The third test ensures that the getMovieById API call does not return anything for an ID we know doesn't exist.

As you can see, you shouldn't only write one unit test when testing a function; you should try to cover at least the following areas:

- Check for existing and non-existing return values

- Check for expected data types

- Check whether the returned values match your expected data

- If you work with ranges, write tests for the edge cases

- If you experienced a bug, reproduce it with a unit test to ensure it will never be encountered again

Writing integration tests with Jest work pretty much the same as unit tests. The difference is that you test larger parts of your application. While the terminology is not always consistent, you can find a good definition in the React Native documentation (https://bit.ly/prn-integration-tests). It counts as an integration test when at least one of the following four points is true:

- Combines several modules of your app

- Uses an external system

- Makes a network call to other applications (such as the weather service API)

- Does any kind of file or database I/O

One thing that is quite important when working with integration tests is mocking. When running tests using Jest as your test runner, you don't have any native parts of your application available; your tests run your JavaScript code in a JavaScript-only environment.

This means you have to *mock* at least all native parts of your application. Jest comes with advanced support for mocking different parts of your code. You can check out the detailed documentation here: https://bit.ly/prn-jest-mocking.

While unit and integration testing work pretty much similar to tests on server applications or applications written in other languages, component tests are a frontend-only test type. This is what we'll look at next.

Working with component tests

When working with component tests in React Native, the recommended solution is to use react-native-testing-library. This library is compatible with Jest, adds a rendering environment for your JavaScript application, and provides multiple useful selectors and other functions.

The easiest type of component test is to check for (unexpected) changes. This is called **snapshot testing**. The component will be rendered and transformed into an XML or JSON representation, called a snapshot. This snapshot is stored with the tests. The next time the test runs, it is used to check for changes.

The following code example shows a snapshot test for the `HomeView` component of our example application:

```
import React from 'react';
import HomeView from '../src/views/home/Home.view';
import {render} from '@testing-library/react-native';
const genres = require('../assets/data/genres.json');
describe('testing HomeView', () => {
  test('HomeView has not changed', () => {
    const view = render(
      <HomeView genres={genres}
                name={'John'}
                onGenrePress={()=>{}}/>,
    );
    expect(view).toMatchSnapshot();
  });
});
```

This code example shows how important it is to take testing into account when structuring your code. We can simply import the `HomeView` component from `Home.view` and pass properties to it when rendering it.

We don't have to mock any stores or external dependencies. This makes it very easy to create the first snapshot test. We use the `render` function from `react-native-testing-library` to create a snapshot representation of the component. Then, we expect it to match our stored snapshot.

While snapshot testing can be very useful to realize unexpected changes, it only gives us information if anything has changed. To get more information about what changed and check whether everything works as expected, we have to create more advanced component tests.

The following code example shows how we can check whether the component renders valid content:

```
test('all list items exist', () => {
  render(<HomeView genres={genres}
                   name={'John'}
                   onGenrePress={() => {}} />);
  expect(screen.getByText('Action')).toBeTruthy();
```

```
  expect(screen.getByText('Adventure')).toBeTruthy();
  expect(screen.getByText('Animation')).toBeTruthy();
});
```

In this test, we pass all three genres we have in our `genres.json` file to the `HomeView` component. Again, we render it using the `render` function from `react-native-testing-library`. After rendering, we use another function from the testing library called `screen`.

With this function, we can query values that are rendered to the simulated screen. This is how we try to find the titles of our three genres, which we expect to be there by checking for them with `toBeTruthy`.

Next, we'll go one step further and check whether we can click on the list items:

```
test('all list items are clickable', () => {
  const mockFn = jest.fn();
  render(<HomeView genres={genres}
                   name={'John'}
                   onGenrePress={mockFn} />);
  fireEvent.press(screen.getByText('Action'));
  fireEvent.press(screen.getByText('Adventure'));
  fireEvent.press(screen.getByText('Animation'));
  expect(mockFn).toBeCalledTimes(3);
});
```

In this test, we use the `fireEvent` function from `react-native-testing-library` to create a press event on every list item. To be able to check whether the press event triggers our `onGenrePress` function, we pass a Jest mock function, created with `jest.fn()`, to the component.

This mock function collects a lot of information during the test, including how often it was called during the test. This is what we check for in this test. However, we can go one step further.

Not only can we check whether the mock function was called, but also whether it was called with the correct parameters:

```
test('click returns valid value', () => {
  const mockFn = jest.fn();
  render(<HomeView genres={genres}
                   name={'John'}
                   onGenrePress={mockFn} />);
  fireEvent.press(screen.getByText('Action'));
  expect(mockFn).toBeCalledWith(genres[0]);
});
```

This example fires only on a press event but then checks whether the arguments that were passed to the function are correct. Since the `Action` genre is the first in the `genres` array, we expect the `onGenrePress` function to be called with it.

Again, these types of tests are only that easy because we have a good code structure. If we hadn't split our home page into a business logic and view, we would have to deal with our navigation library, as well as our global state management solution. While this is possible for most cases, it makes your component tests a lot more complex.

> **Note**
>
> It's a good idea to integrate unit tests, integration tests, and component tests into your CI development process. You should at least run these tests when opening pull requests. If your setup allows, you could also run them on every commit for a faster feedback loop.
>
> I also recommend requiring a certain level of code coverage for the pipelines to pass, to ensure all developers write tests for their code.

All the test types you have learned about so far only use and test parts of your application in a simulated environment. However, that changes when it comes to end-to-end tests.

Understanding end-to-end tests

The idea of end-to-end tests is very simple: these tests try to simulate real-world user behavior and verify that the application behaves as expected. Normally, end-to-end tests work as black-box tests.

This means that the testing framework does not know the inner functionality of the application that is being tested. It runs against the release build of the application, which will be shipped.

Understanding the role of end-to-end testing

At first sight, end-to-end tests seem to be a silver bullet for automated testing. Shouldn't it be enough to simply test all scenarios of our application with end-to-end tests? Do we even need other test types, such as unit tests, integration tests, or component tests?

The answers to these questions are very simple. End-to-end tests are powerful, but they also have some traits that make them only cover certain scenarios very well. First, end-to-end tests run for a long time, so testing all the functionality of a more complex application with end-to-end tests can take up to multiple hours.

This means they can't be run on every commit, which makes the feedback loop much longer. So, this scenario can't be integrated into the CI development process, such as the one described in *Chapter 11, Creating and Automating Workflows*. Second, end-to-end tests are flaky by nature.

This means that these tests can pass and fail on different test runs without any code changes. One reason for this is that applications can behave differently internally, on different test runs. For example, multiple network requests can be resolved in different orders on different test runs.

This is no problem for end users, but it can be for automated end-to-end tests, where you try to run interactions as fast as possible. Another reason for test flakiness is the real-world conditions the tests are running in.

When the testing device has issues with network connectivity while the test runs, the test will fail, even if it should pass. Modern test frameworks try to reduce these problems as much as possible, but they haven't been solved completely.

I recommend using end-to-end tests for the most used paths in your application. This can include account creation and login, as well as the core functionality of your product.

> **Note**
>
> As a developer, you should always ensure there's a balance between ensuring the quality of the product and keeping development speed. Too many end-to-end tests can increase the quality but significantly decrease the speed of your development or release process.

Now that we've looked at end-to-end tests in general, let's start writing our first tests.

Writing end-to-end tests with Detox

Detox is an end-to-end testing framework that was initially developed for React Native applications. It isn't a real black-box testing framework because it injects its own client into the application, which gets tested. This is done to reduce test flakiness, which works quite well but also can't prevent flaky tests completely.

This also means that you don't ship the same binary that was tested. Normally, this should be no problem because you would simply build another binary with the same code and configuration except you would bundle it with the Detox client into your binary, but I wanted to mention it here anyway.

The normal Detox testing process is shown in the following diagram:

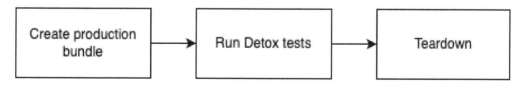

Figure 12.1 – Detox testing process

As you can see, you have to create a production bundle of your application before running your tests. Depending on the machine you create your builds on, as well as the size of your application, this can take some time. Next, you run your tests. After doing so, the testing environment will be torn down so that you can work with the test results.

While this process works fine for running tests, it can be quite annoying while writing tests. Detox works best when using test IDs to identify elements you want to interact with. This means you have to touch your code and add test IDs to these elements.

This also means you have to create a new build every time you have to change anything regarding the test IDs in your code. Fortunately, there is another process you can use while writing your tests. You can also use Detox on development builds, which leads to the following process:

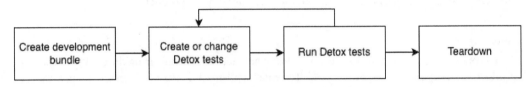

Figure 12.2 – Detox process for writing tests

When working with development builds, you only have to create your native development build once. As you already know, the JavaScript bundle will be fetched from the Metro server running on your computer during development.

This means you can run your tests. If you realize you have to make changes to your test IDs, you can simply apply them and restart your tests. Then, the development build will fetch the new JavaScript bundle from the Metro server and run the tests. This can save a lot of time.

Now that you know Detox in general, let's start working with it. This book does not include a detailed step-by-step guide for installing it since the installation steps changed quite frequently in the past. So, please look at the official installation guide in the Detox documentation here: `https://bit.ly/prn-detox-start`.

If you have trouble getting your Detox tests to work, you can have a look at the example project on GitHub at `chapter-12-detox-testing`.

Writing Detox tests is very similar to writing component tests because Detox uses Jest as its recommended test runner. However, with Detox, we run the test against the real application in a real-world scenario. This means we don't have to work with mocking because everything we need is available. Before we start writing our test, we have to add test IDs to the components we want to interact with.

The following example shows a snippet from `Home.view.tsx`:

```
<Pressable
  key={genre.name}
```

```
    onPress={() => props.onGenrePress(genre)}
    testID={'test' + genre.name}>
    <Text style={styles.genreTitle}>{genre.name}</Text>
</Pressable>
```

Here, you can see the Pressable component, which is used to display the genres. We added a testID property to this component, which makes it identifiable in our tests.

The following code example shows a simple Detox test for our application. You can also find it in the example project repository under e2e/movie.e2e.js:

```
describe('Movie selection flow', () => {
  it('should navigate to movie and show movie details',
  async () => {
    await device.launchApp();
    awaitexpect(element(by.id('testAction'))).
      toBeVisible();
    await element(by.id('testAction')).tap();
    await expect(element(by.id('testmovie0'))).
      toBeVisible();
    await element(by.id('testmovie0')).tap();
    await expect(element(by.id('movieoverview'))).
      toBeVisible();
  });
});
```

First, we tell Detox to launch our app. Next, we wait for the genre with the testAction ID to be visible. Next, we tap the Pressable component. The same is done with the movies, except we don't use the movie names as IDs but the list index. Finally, we verify that the overview text of the movie is shown.

This example shows the advantages and disadvantages of end-to-end testing very well. On the one hand, we only needed a couple of lines of code to navigate to three different screens and verify the content. This means we can be quite confident that the application will not crash on these screens. On the other hand, it takes a lot of time to build the application, load it into a simulator, start it, and run the test.

While Detox can run on real devices, it's mostly used with simulators. These simulators can run in CI environments and therefore be integrated into an automated workflow easily.

But you can even go one step further with end-to-end test integration in your automated workflow. While it is useful to run these tests on simulators, it's even better to run them on real devices. Especially on Android, where you have thousands of different devices, you should at least test the most common ones.

It's not unlikely that some errors will only occur on specific devices or OS versions. Since you don't want to buy hundreds of devices for testing, you can use device farms such as AWS Device Farm. Unfortunately, Detox does not work in these environments, so you have to use Appium as the testing framework. This is what we'll look at next.

Understanding Appium and AWS Device Farm

Unlike Detox, Appium is a real black-box testing framework. It works on your release binary and therefore tests the code you want to ship. It wasn't primarily designed for React Native, but for native Android and iOS testing. Nevertheless, you can use it for React Native apps very well.

Appium is a very mature framework. At the time of writing, version 2 of Appium is still in progress and not ready to use, so the examples here refer to version 1 of Appium.

The framework consists of multiple parts, which you have to understand when working with Appium. The following diagram shows these different parts:

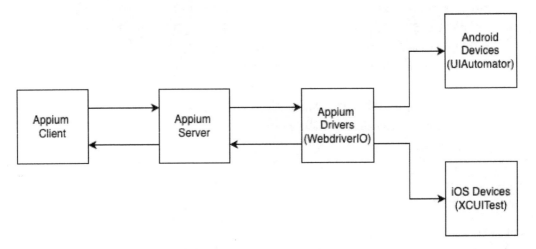

Figure 12.3 – Appium framework components

The core of Appium is a Node.js server, which takes test orders from an Appium client. This client is where you will write your tests. It can be written in different languages such as JavaScript, Java, C#, or Python.

Since you don't want to introduce another language only for writing tests, I recommend going with the JavaScript implementation here. The server then uses an Appium driver to talk to the native testing frameworks, which are used to run the test on real Android and iOS devices.

Appium also provides a desktop application, which has a very useful inspector mode. You can use this mode to find identifiers to write your tests when you don't work with test IDs.

Since the Appium installation process will change significantly with Appium version 2, this book does not contain a detailed step-by-step guide for the installation. You can find these instructions in the official Appium documentation here: `https://bit.ly/prn-appium-installation`.

In my opinion, using Appium with React Native is only interesting when it's combined with a device farm to run your tests on multiple real devices. Otherwise, I would recommend sticking to Detox because it's easier to install, configure, and maintain. But unfortunately, Detox has no support for running on device farms. So, again, you have to use Appium there.

One of these device farms is AWS Device Farm. It is an Amazon service that gives you access to hundreds of different real mobile device models. You can either upload and install your application and use the devices manually via your web browser or you can run automated tests on these devices.

This automated testing is exactly what we'll do. The following diagram shows how the process of running Appium tests on AWS Device Farm integrates with your automated workflow:

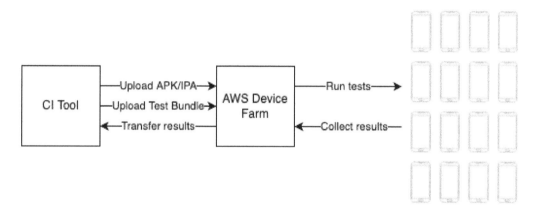

Figure 12.4 – Running automated tests on AWS Device Farm

AWS Device Farm can be accessed programmatically from your workflow automation or CI tool (such as Bitrise) or manually via your web browser. In both scenarios, you have to upload an Android APK or iOS IPA file, which should be tested, and a test bundle.

This bundle is a `.zip` file, which contains the tests as well as some configurations for AWS Device Farm. You can also choose which **device pool** should be used for testing. A device pool is a collection of devices that you can create in the AWS Device Farm console.

AWS then runs your tests on every device that is part of your device pool and collects the test results. These results are displayed in the AWS Device Farm console and can also be passed back to your workflow automation or CI tool.

The following screenshot shows the overview of a test run in AWS Device Farm:

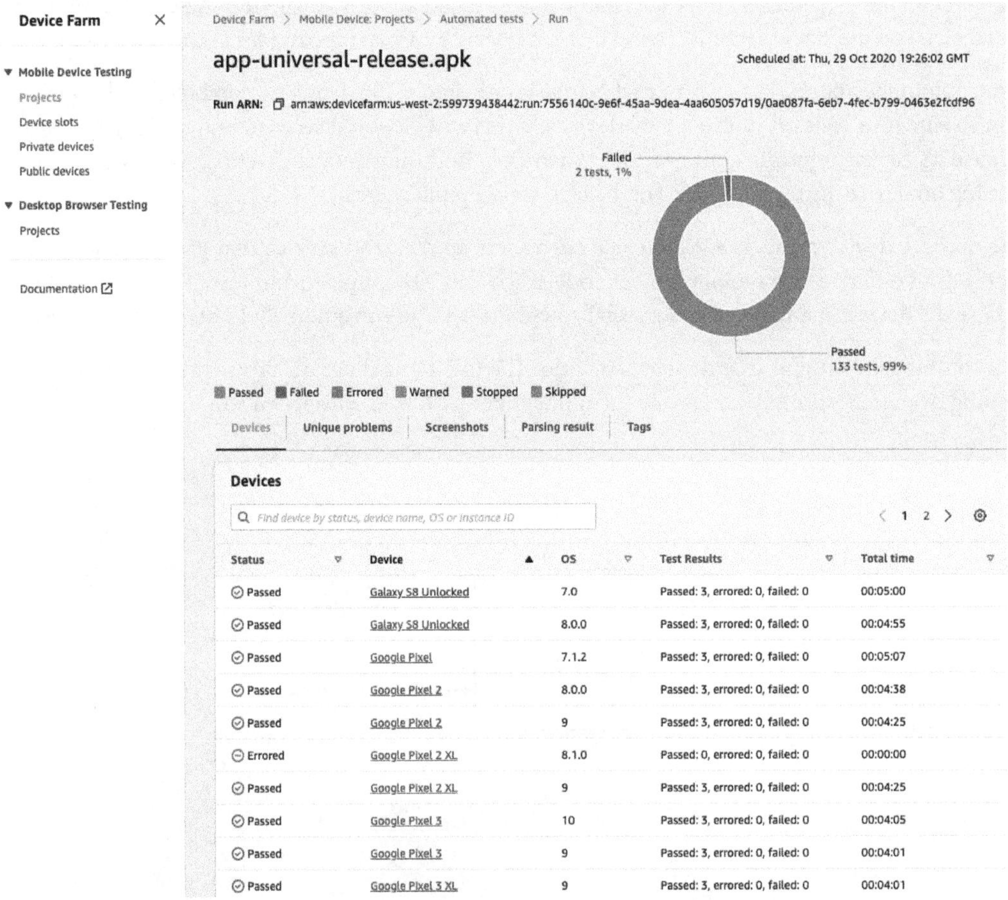

Figure 12.5 – AWS Device Farm result screen

This overview shows a test run that executed three tests on every device of the chosen device pool. All tests passed except two. This means there is either an error that makes two tests fail on one device type, or that two of the tests are flaky.

This is something you would have to investigate. Fortunately, AWS Device Farm provides logs, screenshots, and video recordings of every test run so that you can find out what is happening with ease.

Since the installation and configuration process for using Appium locally and on AWS Device Farm isn't trivial, I created a demo repository that you can start from. It also contains a detailed setup and installation guide, as well as useful scripts for running Appium tests locally and creating bundles for running them on AWS Device Farm. You can find it here: `https://bit.ly/prn-appium-aws-repo`.

Now, let's summarize this chapter.

Summary

First, you learned why automated testing is important and which types of tests exist for React Native apps. Then, you learned how to write unit and integration tests, as well as component tests, with Jest and `react-native-testing`.

Finally, you learned about end-to-end testing while covering two different frameworks: Detox and Appium. After completing this chapter, you should understand that automated testing is an essential part of large-scale projects and that every test type is important because it covers different areas.

Now that you have learned about the basics of writing large-scale applications with React Native, in the last chapter of this book, I will provide some tips from my experience as well as an outlook for the next few years regarding React Native.

13

Tips and Outlook

This chapter is divided into two parts. In the first part, I collected the most useful tips on how to make your React Native project a success. These tips come the things I have learned through a lot of different React Native projects I have worked on as a developer, consultant, software architect, or product owner. I also use React Native as a tech stack in my own companies, where I'm responsible for the business side, so I also know the requirements and pain points of this side.

The second part is an outlook on how I think React Native, its community, and its ecosystem will develop in the future. This is based on its technical development as well as the commitment from different big players in the community.

This means you will learn the following things in this chapter:

- Understanding the most important things to make your React Native project a success
- Understanding the bright future of React Native

Technical requirements

Since this is a completely theoretical chapter, there are no technical requirements.

Understanding the most important things to make your React Native project a success

In this book, you learned a lot about the technical basics of how to ensure a successful React Native project. But if you already worked on production projects, you know that a software project never works as described in the books. There are always obstacles and problems that occur out of the blue and deadlines that seem impossible to meet.

These tips will ensure that you are able to overcome these obstacles, solve these problems, and finally succeed in a real-world software project. So, let's start right away with the tips.

Tip 1 – Find a process you never have to work around

A lot of projects I worked on had clearly defined processes from the beginning, but often, there occurred scenarios where someone worked around the process. A very common example of that is the following:

The business side needs a feature or bugfix to be included in today's release, leading to reduced testing, less detailed reviews, or even direct commits to release branches.

This is something I have experienced in a lot of projects. The problem with this is that in nearly all cases I experienced, it led to a lot more work in the end. The testing has to be done later, bugs that are found have to be fixed anyway, direct commits have to be merged or cherry-picked later, most of the time the code has to be refactored, and in the worst case, a bug can lead to corrupt data that has to be fixed later. So, the work you have with this behavior can easily multiply the work you would have when sticking by the process by 10 times or more.

So, the simple answer would be to say no to the business side, but that's not always possible, because the business side may have a valid concern. Imagine the **chief executive officer** (**CEO**) promised a feature to an important customer and fears not being able to deliver in time because the next release is only in 2 weeks.

This is an example where you have to adapt your process to be able to have faster release cycles or allow urgent releases, to take away the CEO's fears.

This is just an example and a concrete solution for exactly this example. There are multiple other scenarios where team members can lose faith in the process and try to work around it.

Sometimes, it's enough to explain the *why* behind the process; at other times, adaption is needed. But the key takeaway of this subsection is this: *Find a process you trust in and never work around it.*

Tip 2 – Plan to be as flexible as possible with strategies to update without store releases

The bigger the project team is, the more likely it is that something happens that messes up your release planning. Again, I want to start this tip with an example. One application I was working on was translated into 36 languages. This meant that before every release, all texts that were introduced to the **user interface** (**UI**) were passed to translators.

They had 36 hours to translate and verify these texts and upload them to our translation service. After these 36 hours, we ran the release pipeline and released the app with the translations bundled into the binary.

This led to two problems. First, we had to wait 36 hours to be able to pass the release to Apple/Google for review. Second, most of the time, at least one translator was late, resulting in the new texts not being available in that language until the next release.

We solved this problem by adding an update feature for all translations to our application. This feature is illustrated in the following diagram:

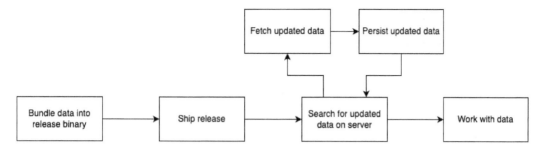

Figure 13.1 – Updating without store release

We still bundle the translation files into the binary and ship the release with these translations, but on app start, we search for updated translations on our server. If we find any, we fetch and persist them locally, to always have the latest version available on the user's device. A more detailed explanation can be found here: `https://bit.ly/prn-update-translations`.

This process not only works for translations but also for any type of data that should be locally available and changes very frequently.

You could even go one step further by using over-the-air update tools such as Microsoft CodePush or Expo Updates. These tools leverage the fact that a React Native app is a native app containing a JavaScript bundle by providing a solution to update the whole JavaScript bundle *over the air*.

Basically, your application connects to the tool's server and searches for an updated JavaScript bundle. If an updated bundle is found, it gets downloaded and your app will start/restart.

While these tools can be very helpful to fix bugs or even improve functionality, it is not allowed to use them to introduce new features due to App Store and Google Play guidelines. Also, you have to keep in mind that they are limited to the JavaScript bundle.

As soon as you introduce new native functionality, assets, or other things, it is not possible to provide such an update with these tools. Even worse, if you try to provide such an update with these tools, you can break your app on the users' devices, because you try to access native functionality that doesn't exist.

So, if you use these tools, be careful. Here, you can read more on CodePush (`https://bit.ly/prn-ms-code-push`), and here, you can find further details of Expo Updates (`https://bit.ly/prn-expo-updates`).

All these ideas have only one goal: to be as flexible as possible to be able to react to any requirements that may occur. Although native releases to App Store or Google Play are no longer a big problem today with Apple and Google getting reviews done in less than 1 day most of the time, it is good to know to be able to deliver updates even if Apple or Google delay the review process.

So, the takeaway of this subsection is this: *Implement a strategy to be able to update your application as fast and flexible as possible.*

Tip 3 – Always be aware of what's happening in your app with stability monitoring tools

There is only one thing that's for sure in software development, and that is that there is no software without bugs. So, your application will contain bugs and users will experience problems with it. The only question is: When will you notice it?

One of the most important things I learned during the last years is that the better you know what's happening in your application, the faster you can respond. The worst case is when you realize a bug only because users write bad reviews about your application.

There are a lot of different stability monitoring tools available as **software-as-a-service** (**SaaS**) products. The most widely used when it comes to React Native apps are Bugsnag and Sentry. Both have excellent support for React Native by providing React Native **software development kits** (**SDKs**).

These SDKs collect native crashes as well as JavaScript errors, add useful information about device type and state, and send them to a server. The server consolidates the data, and the tools provide a web dashboard where you can get information about the stability of your app.

You can have a look at every crash and error and even trace the error back to specific lines in your code by providing source maps.

You can also connect these tools to automatically create issues in your project management tool when a previously unseen bug occurs.

There are other solutions available as well, and you could even write your own, but you should definitely implement any solution to track the stability of your app. So, the takeaway of this tip is this: *Use a stability monitoring tool.*

Tip 4 – Let the user test with A/B testing

A/B testing is something that is used in many areas of mobile app development nowadays, and you should definitely use it too. It means that you divide your users into two groups and provide them with slightly different parts of your application. Then, you wait for a certain time and look at the metrics to see which user group behaves better in the metrics that are important for you.

The most common use case for A/B testing in mobile development is testing new features. If you are not sure if a new feature helps you improve your goal metrics (such as improving retention), you will provide the new feature only to half of your users.

You would tag these users as group *A*. The other users, who have no access to the new feature, would be tagged as group *B*. Then, you would wait and collect data. After some time, you can compare which user group performed better regarding your goal metrics.

This can be done with features, designs, wording, images, and much more. But A/B testing can also be used in completely different cases.

One other example of using A/B testing is releasing an app update to only a group of people. This can be a beta test group, or on Google Play, you can even decide to only roll out your update to a certain percent of your users. You can then compare the stability metrics of the old release and the new release to roll it out to all users.

So, A/B testing can help you get the answers you need in a real-world environment, which is the only environment that counts. So, the key takeaway of this tip is this: *Use A/B testing to collect information to be able to make better decisions.*

Tip 5 – Use TypeScript as a single language stack

TypeScript is a typed language that works on mobile, web, and backend. This is a huge advantage when you set up your project with this single language stack. Your whole team is at least able to read and understand the code of the whole project.

Talented software developers can also transfer from backend to frontend or the other way round if needed, and you can even share code between client and server. This is especially interesting when you have shared data types or business logic that runs on the client for mobile and on the server for web.

Having one shared base for this code guarantees that data types and business logic behavior won't differ between mobile, web, and server.

I experienced the best results, fastest **time to market** (TTM), and best teamwork in projects with this single language stack. So, the takeaway from this tip is this: *Use TypeScript as a single language stack.*

Tip 6 – Keep your code simple and clean

This tip seems to be obvious but let me explain what I mean. There are some simple ideas that keep your code simple and clean.

When working with React and React Native, you often have a lot of different options as to how to solve a specific problem. The first choice you have to make is between functional components or class components.

But there are a lot of other choices to make. Which state management solution do you use? How will you connect your backend? Do you write your own native solutions? If so, which language do you use?

If you make these choices, you should stick to your chosen option. It makes the application more complex if you use functional components and class components for your stateful components. The same applies to all the other options. Make a choice and stick to it.

Next, you should always extract code into components, if you can reuse it anywhere else. Most of the time, it's much easier to create a component with some configuration options instead of writing nearly the same code multiple times.

And most importantly, never duplicate code. This will not only increase the risk of introducing bugs or inconsistencies, but it also will take more time in the long run. Maintaining a lean code base where everything is extracted into components is much easier.

Last, try to write readable code. When completing a feature, always have a look at your code and ask yourself if another developer can understand what you have written without reading any documentation or running the app. If not, try to rename and refactor your code until it's understandable. Write comments if the code doesn't work without these.

The goal is that a new member of your development team can start to be productive as fast as possible. So, the key takeaway here is this: *Write simple, clean, and understandable code with as few different libraries as possible.*

With these tips, you should be able to not only survive but also succeed in your next React Native project.

As the last part of this book, I want to take a brief glimpse into the future of React Native.

Understanding the bright future of React Native

When deciding which technology to use, it always plays an important role in how future-proof this technology is. This is especially important in long-running large-scale enterprise projects. So, I decided to end this book with some arguments as to why you can be absolutely sure that React Native is a good choice.

This is particularly interesting because the last years haven't always been easy for React Native developers. With Flutter, which is based on the very performant **two-dimensional** (**2D**) graphics engine Skia, a new solution for cross-platform development emerged and created a huge hype.

Native development got more and more comfortable with the rise of Kotlin and Swift. React Native in the meantime didn't evolve much. The long-promised refactoring (new architecture), first announced for 2020, took much more time than expected. Some developers started losing faith in React Native.

But this changed in 2022. Now, the future of React Native couldn't be brighter. This is for multiple reasons, which I want to explain in this last section of the book.

Reason 1 – The new architecture has finally landed

As described in *Chapter 3, Hello React Native*, the new architecture brings a huge boost to React Native applications and the React Native community. These are the most important improvements that come with the new architecture:

- **General performance**: The replacement of the old React Native bridge with **JavaScript Interface (JSI)** eliminates the biggest performance bottleneck of React Native. There is no more serialization/deserialization needed when passing data between JavaScript and the native part of your application. This and a lot of other optimizations allow closing the performance gap to Flutter apps or native applications.

- **Startup time**: The new architecture allows lazy loading of the native modules of an application, which improves startup time a lot.

- **Synchronous communication**: With the new architecture, it is now possible to make synchronous calls to native functions from within the JavaScript thread. This can lead to easier and cleaner code.

- **Writing native modules**: CodeGen and the new architecture in general make writing native modules a lot easier. With built-in type safety, it also supports one of the most important features in development.

I expect that the full rollout of the new architecture will be completed by the beginning of 2023. This means that most of the community libraries will be adapted, and you can benefit from all the improvements with your app in a stable environment.

Again, this new architecture is a really big thing because it refutes most of the arguments against using React Native.

The next reason is that there is a new architectural approach to React Native. A community project makes it possible to use Skia in React Native, which is also a huge step forward.

Reason 2 – React Native Skia

As I explained before, Skia is the graphics engine that not only powers Flutter but also Google Chrome, Android, Firefox, and a lot more. Skia is one of the reasons these products have become so popular because it is an extremely powerful and highly performant graphics engine.

There have been some attempts in the past to leverage the power of Skia in React Native, but only with the new architecture was it possible to create a working React Native Skia library. This is another huge boost for React Native because it opens a whole new world when it comes to drawing on your screen.

To understand the extent of the new opportunities with React Native Skia, you have to take a look at how rendering elements in React Native works. As explained in *Chapter 3, Hello React Native*, every component used in the JavaScript code will be mapped to a native component. This also means you can only use the elements and properties that are available on the native side and that have been mapped to React Native components.

React Native Skia uses the same concept but creates a native canvas that can be drawn on with the Skia graphics engine. It then doesn't make native components available in React Native but instead in the Skia **application programming interface (API)**.

This means in the future, you don't have to go with Flutter anymore if you prefer to draw your UI to the screen using your own graphics engine instead of using native components. This is also possible using React Native. You can even use both concepts in the same application.

You should definitely have a look at the project. It is hosted on GitHub; you can find all information here: `https://bit.ly/prn-rn-skia`.

The next reason why React Native has a bright future is as simple as it is important. The community behind the framework is still growing and includes a lot of huge companies that bet big on React Native.

Reason 3 – The community

Even if React Native was initially created by Facebook, React Native is no longer only Meta (formerly Facebook). It is also Microsoft, Shopify, Tesla, Salesforce, Bloomberg, Discord, Coinbase, Pinterest, and a lot more companies.

And these companies are betting big on React Native. Meta is using it in more than 1,000 screens in the Facebook app, which still is one of the most widely used apps in the world. Microsoft uses React Native in some of their most well-known products such as Microsoft Office or Microsoft Teams. The Shopify team rewrote all of their apps in React Native.

And even better, most of these companies not only use React Native, but they are also actively contributing. For example, Microsoft created and maintains React Native for Windows and macOS. Shopify sponsors React Native Skia and supports multiple other community projects such as React Native FlashList.

And it's not only these companies. It is tens of thousands of contributors worldwide. This results in one of the most active developer communities in the world, creating useful, high-quality open source libraries and solutions every day.

Reason 4 – TypeScript and React

While it may not be the right choice for high-performance computing tasks, using TypeScript as the language for your mobile application is absolutely the right choice. You can run it on mobile, web, and server, to share code between these platforms. It is easy to learn and start with, and new developers can get productive very fast.

With TypeScript as your single language stack, you have access to one of the largest talent markets around, much larger than the talent market for Dart (Flutter), Kotlin (native Android), or Swift (native iOS) developers. This is especially important in these times, where **information technology (IT)** talents are very rare.

The same is true for React. It is by far the most used web framework. Every React developer is able to work on React Native projects and can be very productive even after only some days of training. This means you have a really huge talent pool from which you can hire your developing team.

So, you can see that there is nothing to fear when deciding to use React Native in your project. There is a huge commitment to further develop the framework, and you can be absolutely sure that it will be actively maintained for a very long time. Many huge companies are depending on React Native, and they do it for good reasons. So, in my opinion, it is the best choice available to write mobile apps.

Summary

After this outlook, it's time for a short conclusion to this chapter. In the first part of this chapter, you learned how important a good development process is, tips to be as flexible as possible with your releases, how to monitor your apps' stability, how to leverage A/B testing, how to use TypeScript in your mobile application, and how to keep your code simple and clean. In the second part, you got to know the most important reasons why React Native has a bright future and discovered that you can be absolutely sure that it is a good choice for your mobile application.

Now, it's time for final congratulations. You are at the end of this book, and I hope you learned a lot of new and useful things. You should now understand how React Native works and how to use it in large-scale projects to build high-performance apps for multiple platforms, helping you save both time and money.

Index

S

Other Books You May Enjoy

If you enjoyed this book, you may be interested in these other books by Packt:

React and React Native - Fourth Edition

Adam Boduch, Roy Derks, Mikhail Sakhniuk

ISBN: 978-1-80323-128-0

- Explore React architecture, component properties, state, and context
- Work with React Hooks for handling functions and components
- Implement code splitting using lazy components and Suspense
- Build robust user interfaces for mobile and desktop apps using Material-UI
- Write shared components for Android and iOS apps using React Native
- Simplify layout design for React Native apps using NativeBase
- Write GraphQL schemas to power web and mobile apps
- Implement Apollo-driven components

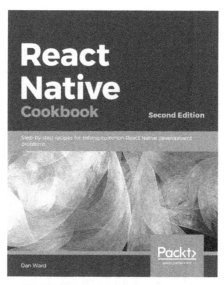

React Native Cookbook - Second Edition

Daniel Ward

ISBN: 978-1-78899-192-6

- Build UI features and components using React Native

- Create advanced animations for UI components

- Develop universal apps that run on phones and tablets

- Leverage Redux to manage application flow and data

- Expose both custom native UI components and application logic to React Native

- Employ open source third-party plugins to create React Native apps

Packt is searching for authors like you

If you're interested in becoming an author for Packt, please visit authors.packtpub.com and apply today. We have worked with thousands of developers and tech professionals, just like you, to help them share their insight with the global tech community. You can make a general application, apply for a specific hot topic that we are recruiting an author for, or submit your own idea.

Share Your Thoughts

Now you've finished *Professional React Native*, we'd love to hear your thoughts! Scan the QR code below to go straight to the Amazon review page for this book and share your feedback or leave a review on the site that you purchased it from.

https://www.amazon.in/review/create-review/error?asin=180056368X

Your review is important to us and the tech community and will help us make sure we're delivering excellent quality content.

Printed in the USA
CPSIA information can be obtained
at www.ICGtesting.com
LVHW080837191223
766860LV00007B/383

9 781800 563681